STE...T
ON ...N

Devotions for High School Graduates

Introduced and compiled by

Kara Lassen Oliver

UPPER
ROOM BOOKS®
NASHVILLE

Library of Congress Cataloging-in-Publication Data

Stepping out on your own : devotions for high school graduates / introduced and compiled by Kara Lassen Oliver.

   p. cm.
  ISBN 978-0-8358-1013-5
  1. High school graduates—Prayers and devotions. 2. High school graduates—Religious life. I. Oliver, Kara.
  BV4850.S743 2009
  242'.63—dc22   2009034013

Printed in the United States of America

Contents

What Do I Do Now?

PART 2: LISTENING FOR GOD

Where Do I Belong?

Preparing for My New Life: Beyond What I See

Looking Ahead

Introduction

Congratulations, graduate! You made it!

You may have soared through high school, graduating with academic honors, sports accolades, trophies, and an amazing list of accomplishments. Or maybe you slogged through each day, surprising your parents by graduating, and managing to avoid any piece of paper or memento with your high school logo on it. Whether you feel that high school was the high point of your life or you think anything else would be better, I welcome you to this new journey and adventure.

You are about to move into a new era of independence that will include amazing freedom and equally amazing responsibility. You will have to say good-bye—or good riddance—to some people, comforts, and burdens. And you have the opportunity to explore and embrace new relationships, opportunities, and challenges. I hope that you know you do not travel alone. Not only do you follow in the footsteps of thousands of graduates before you but also in the steps of ancestors of your faith. You have left the familiar to step out into the new and the unknown.

As you step into your future, you go with God's blessing and God's promise: "I will guide you along the best pathway for your life. I will advise you and watch over you" (Psalm 32:8, NLT).

These days, weeks, or months after high school are a gift of time to reflect on where you have been. They also give you a chance to contemplate and discern where and how you will go forward. Whether you enter the workforce, take time to travel, head to college, join the military, or commit to mission and service in the world, you will need to leave behind some things and pick up new ones.

As you read through the devotions in this book, I invite you to consider your journey in three stages:

1. As you leave high school and your home, or as your friends move away from you, consider what you need to release and give to God.

2. As you spend time in God's presence, consider what wisdom you hear from God in prayer and in the witness of scripture and other disciples.

3. As you move into the next phase of your journey, consider how you can use your unique gifts to serve God in the world.

You will walk through these stages many times in your life. The journey of discipleship involves constant release, listening, and integration of new hurts, joys, "aha" moments, and setbacks.

May you find in these pages words that speak to your individual experience and join you to the common journey of all those who seek to live faithfully.

Part 1

[LEAVE-TAKING]

SAYING GOOD-BYE

Imagine standing at the front door of your high school, facing the outdoors. Take several deep breaths, and ask for God's presence, peace, and comfort to be made known to you.

Then see yourself taking that first step into the outdoors, away from high school and into your future. As you move forward, who will continue to walk alongside you? Whom will you have to leave behind?

What experiences give you strength for the journey? What pulls you back to the comfort and familiarity of life in high school? This push-and-pull is a natural and unavoidable part of any transition in life. There will be anxiety and exhilaration, struggle and new energy.

As you read the scriptures and pray the prayers in the following pages, be honest about your own feelings and vulnerable to God's love and calling. You may want to make notes or journal about your thoughts, fears, and hopes.

Sanctuary

The sun beats down.
I am hot and tired.
I fear being trampled by trials
    in my way.
Disappointment and sadness
    surround me.
I need to escape to a place—
    cool and quiet,
    a rest, a shade from the
    heat of the day.
You, Lord, offer sanctuary.
You draw me close.
You fill my cup. Let it overflow!
Let it splash me, wash me,
    refresh me.
You, Lord, offer a quiet place
    to close my eyes and breathe.
Thank you, God, for
    peaceful escape.

Rebecca Pacuch, 21 [Kissimmee, Florida]

[Journal: Write about the fears, disappointments, and
sadness that surround you during this time of transition.
Where do you find the cool and quiet sanctuary of
God's presence?]

You have taught me since I was a child,
and I never stop telling about your marvelous deeds.
Psalm 71:17 (CEV)

When I Grow Up

Have you wondered when you will stop saying, "When I grow up . . ."? We seem to think that life begins at a certain age and that we can't do much until then. But God has put us in a specific place, at a particular time; and that time is now. God has a plan for this part of our lives as well as for our lives ten years from now.

We have the idea that until we outgrow our curfew, get married, and work full-time, our lives haven't really started. We expect that when we reach the age of eighteen or twenty-one, we will suddenly be grown-up—and then we can be "perfect Christians."

Someday we will look back on our youth and wonder why we didn't give our lives to God earlier. If we don't pursue God now, we may not follow God when we're grown. Let's live today as we want to live our entire lives because, believe it or not, our lives have already begun.

Shelby Stuart, 19 [Atascadero, California]

Journal: Finish the sentence, "When I grow up. . . ." What things have you been putting off until you get older? As you leave childhood behind, how do you have new freedom to pursue the things on your list?

"For I know the plans I have for you," declares the LORD, "plans to prosper you and not to harm you, plans to give you hope and a future."
Jeremiah 29:11 (NIV)

God's Dream

Do you remember your first dream of what you wanted to be when you grew up? When I was little, I wanted to be a veterinarian. Now that I am getting ready for college, my dreams have changed. I look forward to majoring in music.

I changed my mind because God called me. When I was in eighth grade, I attended a Christian choir camp and fell in love with music. My hope is to serve God by using my voice.

Following my dream and what I believe is God's will for my life hasn't been easy. In the middle of my sophomore year of high school, I had to transfer to a new school in order to study in a better music program. I've spent hours in music lessons and even more hours practicing. I've had to be incredibly focused.

Although following my dream hasn't been easy, it has been fun. Every time I sing, I thank God for the gift of music. No other dream makes me happier than the one God has for my life.

Kaitlin M. Schneider, 18 [Monroe, Michigan]

[
Reflect: Have some of your earlier dreams been replaced by new, bigger, or better dreams? How did that transition happen? Do you feel like this is a time for new dreams?
]

The LORD your God is with you,
  he is mighty to save.
He will take great delight in you,
  he will quiet you with his love,
  he will rejoice over you with singing.
Zephaniah 3:17 (NIV)

My Dad's Blessing

"May the peace, presence, and love of our Lord Jesus Christ protect, strengthen, inspire, and guide you all the days of your life." Since the day I was born, my dad has offered this prayer for me every night as he tucked me into bed. By doing so, he has taught me that my destiny lies not in his hands or in my own but in the more capable hands of God. No one on earth knows my destiny; but the peace, presence, and love of God will prepare me for it.

And because of my dad's daily blessing, I am more aware of God's protection, power, inspiration, and guidance at work in my life; and this makes me even more excited and confident about my future. Sometimes I worry about what it will be like when my dad won't be there to bless me, but every night I remember that God has a plan for my life and will be there to guide me into the future.

Kelsey Kordella, 16 [Pittsburgh, Pennsylvania]

> **Prayer:** God, I offer to exchange the worries I have about my destiny for the opportunity to journey with you, even into an unknown future. Help me to seek your direction and to follow with obedience, always trusting in your love and your plans for me.
>
> **Charles T. Ware, 19** [Arcadia, Florida]

Discovery

You want to be an eagle,
independent,
strong,
unfettered by adolescent fears.

But as you try to fly
in proud spirals that move higher and higher,
you look down and cry
one cry.

For a moment,
feeling the panic of soaring
without knowing how to land,
you flutter ineffectually
until the wind catches up;
and the glorious lift of air under wings
overcomes fear.

For the moment,
the flight is enough.
When it's time to land,
you will learn.

Melinda Williams [Box Elder, South Dakota]

[
Reflect: As you move into this new phase of your
life, what panics or scares you? What makes you feel
strong and independent?
]

In you, O LORD, I take refuge; . . .
Be to me a rock of refuge,
    a strong fortress, to save me,
    for you are my rock and my fortress.

Psalm 71:1, 3 (NRSV)

My Fortress

Plagued by doubt and anxiety,
focused on the future or past,
    the present isn't important.
Concerned about school, grades, friends,
relationships that can't survive the storm,
    you'd find my complaints trivial.
They pass in weeks; and I forget in time,
directing my attention to another
    fleeting interest of this world.
But you are there, never changing—
    my strength and peace,
    the certainty in my changing,
        whirling world—
begging to hold and cradle me,
longing to take away all fear
and to replace it with your light.

Catherine Howard, 16 [Kernersville, North Carolina]

[
Reflect and Rejoice
A mighty fortress is our God,
    a bulwark never failing;
our helper he amid the flood
    of mortal ills prevailing.

—**Martin Luther**, "A Mighty Fortress Is Our God"
]

LIVING IN LIMBO

Often in life we make progress toward our goals, only to experience some type of setback or delay. The distance that at first seemed short continues to stretch out before us, despite the time that has passed.

As a recent graduate, you may feel as though you are living in a "two-steps-forward-one-step-back" time, living in the now and the not-yet. You are currently a graduate, but you aren't yet a college student, or you haven't started doing whatever you plan to do. You want independence, but you haven't yet left home. You are ready to begin your new life, but your daily life looks much the same.

Living in limbo can be frustrating and may seem endless. But this in-between time can also be a gift, offering you opportunities for rest and discernment before new commitments and responsibilities take hold of your life.

Try to appreciate the gift of the forward and backward movement of your journey.

Wait, Trust, Act

Do you wish you could see yourself ten years from now?
I do. I wonder: *What college will I attend? Whom will I
marry? What career will I choose?*

As a Christian, I desire God's direction for my life. All
too often, though, I get impatient and charge ahead on my
own, making a mess of things. Patience is not easy for me,
and I certainly am not good at waiting; but I'm finding that
God's plans are worth waiting for.

Lamentations 3:25-26 (NIV) says, "The LORD is good to
those whose hope is in him, to the one who seeks him; it is
good to wait quietly for the salvation of the LORD." Don't be
impulsive. Give your future to the Lord every morning, and
wait patiently. Of course, waiting for the Lord doesn't mean
loafing on the couch and expecting God to do everything
for you. It means waiting for God to offer opportunities and
trusting God to guide you as you make decisions and take
action.

Psalm 119:105 (NIV) says that God's Word is "a lamp to
my feet and a light for my path." I'm learning that God rarely
turns on the brights to let me see what's way up ahead, but
the Lord does give me light for each step along the way.

Isa Adney, 19 [Debary, Florida]

Learn to Wait
We must learn to wait,
to acquire the ability
to set time aside,
to live in the here and now
and not hurry the yet-to-come,
for patience is a virtue.

K. S. Hardy [Bowling Green, Ohio]

[Moses said to the Israelites]
"The eternal God is your refuge,
     and underneath are the everlasting arms."
Deuteronomy 33:27a (NIV)

Swimming Lessons

Every summer when I was little, my family vacationed at a small lake in northern Illinois. One of my fondest memories is the day Dad taught me to swim. From my five-year-old perspective, that little lake seemed as large as an ocean; and I was scared.

"Relax," Dad said. "Just lie on your tummy, and the water will hold you up."

"What if it doesn't?" I asked nervously. "What if I sink? What if I drown?"

"My arms will always be underneath you," Dad promised. "I'll never let you drown."

At first, every time I tried to float, I would tense up and begin to sink. Then I would feel Dad's strong arms underneath me. Reassured, I would relax and float back to the surface. Eventually, I learned not only to swim but also to enjoy swimming.

Years later, when I read Deuteronomy 33:27 for the first time, I knew exactly what the verse meant. I could still remember the reassuring feeling of Dad's strong arms beneath me as I learned how to swim. Now, whenever I face a challenge, I remind myself that God is always with me, holding me up with everlasting arms. Even if my problem seems as big as the ocean, my heavenly Father will never let me drown.

Linda Hentschel [Lebanon, Ohio]

You, LORD, are the light that keeps me safe.
I am not afraid of anyone.
 You protect me, and I have no fears.
Psalm 27:1 (CEV)

Basket of Worries

Imagine a big picnic basket falling from the clouds and landing near you. A voice calls out in the middle of all the stress of a busy day: "Come, put your worries inside my basket." You reach into the depths of your mind and take out all the troubles that are weighing you down. Then you open the basket and place your worries inside. You feel lighter, relieved. A hand reaches down from the sky, taking the basket and the worries to heaven, where they belong. This was the image my mom taught me to picture in my mind when I had a serious problem with worrying.

The Bible also tells us to give all our worries to God. (Check out Psalm 55:22.) We shouldn't worry; God will provide for us. If we give our cares to God, we will have more time and energy to serve God and to enjoy life.

Lara Hulbert, 15 [Ann Arbor, Michigan]

Try This: Draw a picture of your own basket of worries. What worries have you already released to God? Which ones are you still firmly grasping? Pray that God will help you loosen your grip on these worries. Then imagine God lifting this basket of worries from you.

Whatever you do, whether in word or deed, do it all in the name of the Lord Jesus, giving thanks to God the Father through him.

Colossians 3:17 (NIV)

Step-by-Step

Some people have always known their calling. Since they were young, they've wanted to be firefighters, doctors, or missionaries. I am not one of those people. Some people have obvious skills, talents, or dreams that point them in a specific direction. I don't.

I'd love to know exactly where I'm headed. I'd love to map out my future: college, jobs, finances, relationships. I'd love to know my destiny. But despite my careful plans, life is unpredictable. Each time I get caught up in planning the details, God seems to say, "Slow down."

Yet God remains faithful; and little by little, I'm learning to trust. I may not have a clear picture of what I'll be doing a year from now, but I know what I'm doing today. As long as I follow God step-by-step, God will take care of my future.

Cherith Long, 22 [Mansfield, Texas]

5-Second Prayer: Thank you, God, for walking with me each step, little by little, into the future.

So Little Time

Be still
> Slow down.
> Don't rush.
> Don't worry.
> Don't focus on tomorrow
>> or yesterday
>> or even today.
> Instead, breathe.
> Be here.
> Be now.
>> This moment,
>> this place,
>> this experience
>>> is waiting for your noticing.

and know
> Learn.
> Understand.
> Believe.
> Own.
> Immerse yourself in the power.

that I
> I,
> myself,
> me,

am

> created to be,
> can be in the image of

God.

Melinda Williams [Box Elder, South Dakota]

> **Reflect:** In your life, what could it mean to "be still, and know that I am God"?

Hope Begins Again

The rains came;
and all was washed away,
buried under gallons of water,
cleansed beyond clean.
And in the end,
after forty days and forty nights,
Noah floated right along.
And the world began again.

The earth shook,
and all was swallowed up
in one huge gulp
to fill the empty hole
below.
And in the stillness after,
the sound of children's laughter
rose on the wind.
And life began again.

The heat scorched the land;
and all was parched and dry,
burning up inside,
deaf to thirsting cries.
Yet lying in wait,
new life in place
pushed up through dust to open space.
And growth began again.

Darkness fills my sight;
and all that's left to fight
is within me,
seeking a glimmer of light.
Night hides hope in the shadows,
and the scope of pain seems too much;
yet dawn breaks through as grace from you.

Melinda Williams [Box Elder, South Dakota]

[**Be Hopeful:** Whom do you know who has said good-bye to a present reality to step into an unknown but beautiful future?]

Chaos

When I think about my future and what the rest of my life will hold, my mind starts going a hundred miles an hour! It's not that I don't know what I want to do; it's that I don't know which idea I should choose. There are so many opportunities and hopes and wishes floating around in my head that I don't know what I want to do the most.

But I have confidence that God will lead me in the direction that God wants me to go. I feel pulled toward countless things that have nothing to do with each other, but I know that many of those desires and goals are completely selfish and will not glorify God. I have spent my growing-up years filling my head with things I'd like to do and places I'd like to see. Right now I can hardly make sense of anything.

Yet, I know that in this chaos, God will prevail and will show me how to "live a life worthy of the calling" that I will receive. But until I know my specific calling, "I press on" (Philippians 3:12, NIV) and have faith that God is leading me.

Christy Lee, 17 [Winston-Salem, North Carolina]

[
Press On: Do you feel confused about where God may be leading you or about what God may be calling you to do? Look up Philippians 3:12 and reflect on what it means to "press on" in the midst of chaos.
]

Find out what Jesus thinks about uncertainty in Matthew 6:25-34.

An Eternal Perspective

I tend to second-guess everything. I often wonder if I've chosen the right college. When I drive across a pothole, I worry about possible car damage. After dressing, I stare into the mirror, afraid that everyone, including the girl I am trying to impress, will look at my clothes and regard me as a loser. The list goes on and on.

From the mundane routine of our everyday lives to the bigger issues such as terrorism, there is certainly a lot to be uncertain about. But if we view life from an eternal perspective, our uncertainties can lose their anxious qualities. If we recall Jesus' words of comfort about God's feeding the birds of the air and clothing the lilies of the field, it is easier to deal with life's uncertainties.

It's not easy to keep an eternal perspective about life; but when I do, I realize that no matter what I am uncertain about, God is in control and will take care of me.

Ralph Asher, 19 [Hebron, Indiana]

[
Just a Thought
From heaven even the most miserable life will look like one bad night at an inconvenient hotel.
—Saint Teresa of Avila, Spain, 16th century
]

"I am the LORD your God,
who teaches you what is best for you,
who directs you in the way you should go."
Isaiah 48:17b (NIV)

Next Steps

My friends and I are busy taking the SAT, studying for tests, applying for scholarships, and writing essays for college applications. However, like many other high school seniors, we haven't quite figured out our next steps. We may know what career we want to pursue, but where will we go to college—and how will we pay for it? What will life be like when we are no longer in high school?

Starting over after high school can be scary. I'm making plans to study engineering at a college in Michigan, but who knows what I'll be doing this time next year? God may have different plans for me; and my goal is to be the kind of person who will lay aside my work and my plans to follow God's plans, because I know they will be awesome!

Rachel Spoelman, 17 [Penang, Malaysia]

Prayer: God, what do you want me to do with my life? How will I know if I am making the right choices? I worry that I am not on the path you desire for me. Still, your Spirit calms my soul. Your Word reassures me that you will guide me in the way I should go. Thank you, Lord. Amen.

Some People Who Wondered What Was Next
- Noah: Genesis 6:9–7:5
- Abraham: Genesis 12:1-9
- Moses: Exodus 3:1–4:23; 5:1-2
- Amos: Amos 9:1-8
- Jonah: Jonah 1:1–3:5
- Jesus' Disciples: Matthew 4:18-22; 9:9, 19

Worry-Free

I am a self-professed worrywart. In my daily battle against worry, these remedies help me the most:

Praying
When I am honest and tell God my worries, they no longer control me. I talk with other Christians, and they pray for me too. My Sunday school class and my e-mail prayer partner provide me with prayer support.

Reading the Bible
I learn what the scripture teaches about worry. Jesus commands, "Do not worry about your life" (Matthew 6:25a, NIV). Paul instructs, "Do not be anxious about anything, but in everything, by prayer and petition, with thanksgiving, present your requests to God" (Philippians 4:6, NIV). Reading the Bible reminds me to trust God instead of dwelling on my problems.

Changing My Focus

If I am worried, doing something different changes the focus of my thoughts. Watching a movie, reading a book, or calling a friend often does the trick. Exercise is another way to divert the restless energy that promotes worry. I like to row on our rowing machine, punch a punching bag, or take my dog for a walk.

Writing in a Journal

I write the worries out of my system. I write about my fears, and I also write down plans that will help resolve my troubles. In this way my worrying leads to action.

Elizabeth Irby [Hillsboro, Oregon]

Reflect: Choose one thing that is worrying you. What is your prayer? What wisdom do you find in scripture? What can you do to change your focus? Journal your answers to each question.

MOVING AWAY

Remember the last time you moved to a new place, or imagine a future move. As you start out, you can still see your house in the rearview mirror. As you lose sight of your house, you are still among familiar streets and sights. But as you get on the highway and leave town, the scenery is new, maybe appealing or maybe unsettling. Having never been there before, you may lose confidence in your directions or the time it will take to reach your destination. In a new place

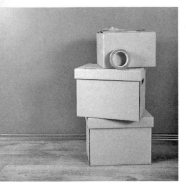

it takes time to reorient yourself, to feel at home.

Whether you are moving to an apartment across town or to a new country, you face the challenge of reorienting your perspective. Who goes with you for coffee when your best friend is in a different city? If you're still living at home, how do you move into greater freedom and fewer rules with your parents? When can you have devotional time if your roommate never leaves the dorm room? What do you do when you miss your old life? And how do you embrace the new location of your body, mind, and spirit?

As you take time for devotions in the coming weeks, be patient with yourself as you reorient yourself to the changes in your life.

[God says] "I am with you and will watch over you wherever you go."
Genesis 28:15a (NIV)

Leaving Home

As I write this, it's July and I'll be off to college in less than a month. Last week one of my sisters (we're triplets) helped me clean out my closet and sort through my clothing. Yesterday I spent the day packing up music and books. The sense that I was moving away from Spencer, New York, became more real. When I've attended camps or taken trips, Spencer has always been my final destination, my home. Now a new place will become my home. I'll always be able to come back to Spencer, but it will be different. My sisters and friends may not be here, and the people I knew when I was growing up will all be older. My college community will be my home, at least for the next four years.

I'm sad about leaving my sisters, who have always been a part of me; my parents, who have always been a source of encouragement and comfort; and my friends. But I'm excited as I look forward to meeting people with different experiences, to taking part in challenging activities, and to finding my place in a new intellectual community. I am also at peace, knowing that God will always be right beside me, leading me.

Elizabeth Campbell, 19 [Spencer, New York]

[
Just a Thought
It's interesting to leave a place, interesting even to think about it. Leaving reminds us of what we can part with and what we can't, then offers us something new to look forward to, to dream about.
—Richard Ford, *Harper's Magazine* (Feb. 1992)
]

Be patient, bearing with one another in love. Make every effort
to keep the unity of the Spirit through the bond of peace.
Ephesians 4:2b-3 (NIV)

Fly Away Home

"She grew up in one seven-hour flight." That's what my
family said about me a few years ago. Two months after
finishing high school, I was on a plane to London, England,
where I would stay for a year as a full-time volunteer for an
organization called Time for God.

In just a few days, I had bid farewell to my old life and
had begun a new life in a foreign country. The task was
challenging and forced me to learn independence. For the
first time in my life, I was on my own. I was my own boss. Yet
I still talked to my family; and I realized, in my absence, how
much they meant to me.

After my year of service, I moved back to the United
States and back home with my family. Even though I had
lived on my own, my parents still worried about me and set
rules for me. Coming home wasn't easy, but I wouldn't have
had it any other way. And now, breaking away for good
won't be so bad, knowing that my family will be there for me
when I need a place to come home to.

Kari Duffy, 20 [Millbury, Ohio]

Prayer: Thank you, God, for watching over us when we
are on our own and for giving us a place to call home.
Amen.

I have become
   like a bird alone on a roof.
Psalm 102:7b (NIV)

Lonely

Today I am lonely,
    lonely as can be.
No one to talk to,
    nothing on TV.
Locked in a room of loneliness,
I can't find the key.

I've cleaned my room 23 times;
I've counted my money—19 pennies, 29 dimes.
The sun shines bright, but my head hangs low.
I've painted my nails, even my toes.
God, please help me,
    for I am still bored!

I've called my friends on the telephone.
Nobody answers.
Nobody's home.
As I lie in bed thinking what to do,
I wonder,
Is anyone as lonely as I am?
    Are you lonely too?

Leticia Mickey, 22 [Gibsonia, Pennsylvania]

Try This: When you are as lonely as a bird on a roof,
remember that God is with you. "Even the sparrow finds
a home . . . at your altars, O LORD" (Psalm 84:3, NRSV).

The LORD your God will be with you wherever you go.
Joshua 1:9 (NIV)

Moving

I've moved seven times in twenty years, and it's tough. But I've learned some ways to cope with separation. Maybe they will help you too.

- Sometimes I have a good cry. Jesus wept. So did King David, as well as many of God's prophets and the apostle Paul. Why shouldn't I?

- I keep in touch with family and friends. I'm glad for letters, phone calls, e-mail, instant messages, Facebook, photos, and video cameras.

- I ask God to lead me to new places where I can be involved in ministry and meet new friends.

Moving to a new place is stressful. It takes a while to fit in. But God has always led me to become an active part of each new community.

Rich Maffeo [Gales Ferry, Connecticut]

Trust God
Are you about to go separate ways from one of your best friends? God is the keeper of friendships across the miles. Rest assured that the palm of God's hand is a safe place to keep your friendship.

Amanda Hanson, 21 [Hamilton, Illinois]

[Jesus said,] "I have called you friends, for everything that I learned from my Father I have made known to you."
John 15:15b (NIV)

Letters from Home

After my high school graduation, I left home to become an exchange student in the Netherlands. This had been my dream for years, so I was surprised when the homesickness hit. I missed my friends and struggled to make new ones. Letters from home were comforting. At first, I received tons of mail; but as time passed, only my closest friends kept writing. I was lonely.

As a brand-new Christian, I hadn't yet developed the habit of daily Bible reading. But someone had given me a paperback New Testament before I left home, and I was so bored and lonely that I decided to read it. As I read, I discovered that the Bible was like a letter from a friend. My loneliness eased, and I began to enjoy my time in the Netherlands.

One year later, I packed to return home. Into my suitcase went a bundle of letters from faithful friends, an album with pictures of my new Dutch friends, and a well-worn New Testament, dingy and dog-eared, with the best parts underlined.

After several years, I'm still in touch with the friends I made in the Netherlands. And every day I read my Bible, which is like getting a letter from my dearest friend.

Linda Hentschel [Lebanon, Ohio]

Pen Pals: Commit with at least one other friend to check in with each other once a week. Tell stories and share prayer requests.

The LORD came and stood there, calling as at the other times, "Samuel! Samuel!" Then Samuel said, "Speak, for your servant is listening."

1 Samuel 3:10 (NIV)

Open to God's Call

It's been over a year since I traveled to China, and I still marvel at all I learned. Last summer, God opened doors and hearts, including mine, and led me to Ningbo, China. For six weeks, I served as an English teacher to forty-four Chinese children.

When I left for China, I had doubts. I didn't speak Chinese. I couldn't eat with chopsticks. I wasn't a certified teacher. Then I read the story of Samuel's call in 1 Samuel 3. God had a special purpose for Samuel, and Samuel trusted God. He was open to the Lord's leading. After reading the scripture, I knew that I had all I needed to travel to China—a willingness to follow God's direction.

Because I was open to God's service, I experienced an exciting culture and formed lasting friendships with people half a world away. And because I was open, God opened doors so that I could proclaim the gospel.

May I always be open to God's leading and answer willingly, "Here I am, Lord."

Kristen Barz, 21 [San Antonio, Texas]

[
Reflect: Think of an area of your life in which you feel challenged to move out of your comfort zone. What would it take for you to be able to say, "Here I am, Lord"?
]

WHAT DO I DO NOW?

In our daily lives, there are always tasks to accomplish, forms to fill out, shopping lists to make, and physical needs to attend to. Important and necessary tasks can sometimes distract us from the goals they serve. It is easy to miss the beautiful journey God has for us when we are looking down at lists and e-mails. Raise your eyes so you can enjoy the journey and appreciate the view from where you are.

As you enter your devotional time, think about whether you have been aware of God's presence in your life. How do you take time to appreciate God's presence in each task, decision, and step?

Turning Away

Every morning as I kneel by my bed,
I pray that you will take my heart.
I pray you'll lead me and will walk ahead.
I pray, God, for a brand-new start.
Since I cannot know what you have in store,
I pray you'll guide me every day.
Yet every time you open up a door,
I shake my head and turn away.

I think that I know better than you do
'bout what should happen in my life.
I drop you hints and try to send you clues
that fame and fortune might be nice.
You guide me better than the northern star,
yet I see that the end is near.
I become proud that I have come this far,
and I forget who brought me here.

I feel that I no longer need your hand.
I take whatever path I choose.
Then when things don't go just as I had planned,
I turn and blame it all on you.
I need to learn that you have so much more
in store for me than just today.
Yet every time you open up a door,
I shake my head and look away.

Christina Dotson [North Fairfield, Ohio]

[
Think About It: What keeps you from walking through
the doors God opens for you?
]

In all your ways acknowledge [God],
and he will make your paths straight.

Proverbs 3:6 (NIV)

Questions

What is my calling?
Is there something specific
I've been called to do?

Which path do I take?
There are so many choices.
Which one do I choose?

Is there really One who can guide me,
help me make the right choice?
If God is really out there calling me,
why can't I hear that voice?

When will I be given a sign?
How do I know when to take a chance?
Can that serenity be mine?
When do I let go, let my heart dance?

What is my calling?
Which path do I take?
What choice will leave me falling?
Which decision shall I make?

Courtney Thompson, 20 [Spring, Texas]

[**Pray:** God, there are so many choices in front of me
and so many decisions to make! May I feel assurance
that you are with me and will guide my path. Amen.]

The Lord and the Spirit are one and the same, and the Lord's Spirit sets us free. So our faces are not covered. They show the bright glory of the Lord, as the Lord's Spirit makes us more and more like our glorious Lord.

2 Corinthians 3:17-18 (CEV)

Reflecting on God

As I've considered what career path to choose, I have spent a lot of time trying to figure out who I am and what I most like to do. It would be easier if God would simply spell out what I should do with my life.

Despite my uncertainty about careers, I know that God wants my life to reflect God's glory. When I think of reflecting God, I think of a pure, white snowfall reflecting sun. The light of the sun is blinding when magnified by the snow.

God is like the sun, bathing me with light. I am like the snow. The purer my life is, the more I will be able to reflect God's light to others. The more I reflect God—by showing kindness to a difficult person or even by having patience in a checkout line—the more I become the person God created me to be. And as that happens, I imagine choosing a career will be much easier.

India Cable, 23 [Madison, Indiana]

Reflect God's Light
God shines light for all of us
that we may clearly see
the way to live, the path to take—
the signs are clear when we believe.

Linda Sackett-Morrison [Franklin, Michigan]

Whoever speaks must do so as one speaking the very words of God; whoever serves must do so with the strength that God supplies, so that God may be glorified in all things through Jesus Christ. To him belong the glory and the power forever and ever. Amen.

1 Peter 4:11 (NRSV)

Me or Thee?

Lord, I have to confess that
many times my hopes and dreams
have to do with being popular
    and being noticed
or making lots of money
    and being successful
    in the eyes of the world.

But lately I'm seeing that
the hopes and dreams you bless
have to do with being obedient
    and becoming all you've called me to be.
These hopes and dreams
    have you, not me, at their center.
They are about bringing you, not me, glory.
They are about lifting up your name
    and not my own.

Deliver me from my desire
    to have everyone notice me.
Instead let my goal be
    that everyone will notice you
       in me.

Elaine Creasman [Largo, Florida]

5-Second Prayer: Lord, be at the center of my hopes and dreams.

I will point out the road
    that you should follow.
I will be your teacher and watch over you.
Psalm 32:8 (CEV)

Who Do You Want to Be?

"What do you want to be when you grow up?" That's the question grown-ups have been asking me since I was in preschool. Then, I thought that anything was possible; and I embraced the future with open arms. Now I am biding my time, uncertain and a bit afraid of what the future holds.

What if I wake up one day twenty years from now, look around, see the new car and the big house that classify me as successful, and realize that I'm not passionate about what I am doing? What if I get sucked into the cycle of an ordinary everyday job, if all my childhood dreams get washed down the drain like rotting fruit?

I expressed these fears to my big sister, who has helped me to grow up and to think about my future.

She replied, "It's not what you want to be that's important; it's *who* you want to be."

A career will not determine my personality, just as grades and physical attributes don't determine who I am and how I feel now. Who I am when I grow up will determine what I do.

I'm not scared anymore. I've decided who I want to be: a follower of Jesus Christ. And I trust that God will guide me and give me gifts and talents that lead me to a career.

Virginia Thomas, 14 [Asheville, North Carolina]

[Journal: Write words that describe who you want to be when you grow up.]

A Prayer for Discernment

Amidst "the forest of my own wanderings"
I see the path that has brought me here—
　　beautiful, manicured, and solid.
I have walked with giants and saints
　　who have inspired me to seek more.
I stand in a clearing now
　　as if at the heart of God.
I bask in the holy stillness,
　　uncertain of the next step,
But certain that the path
　　no longer meanders, but strides
　　　　into the future.

Lord, grant me humility to embrace
　　a path I did not choose,
To view obedience as illumination,
To walk with confidence this life of
　　radical discipleship
　　In order to be transformed
　　into the likeness of Christ.

Kara Oliver [blog.oliverville.org, posted September 7, 2008]

Say a Prayer: When you're feeling confused about the decisions you have to make, remember God's guidance in the past, and seek God in the present so that you may stride forward with confidence.

Isaiah 41:9-10 assures us that God chooses, calls, and guides us.

Called

All Christians are called to be in relationship with God and with other believers, to grow spiritually, and to evangelize. However, God has given each person unique skills, gifts, and talents to use to fulfill these purposes.

God has been revealing my calling a little bit at a time. Early on, God let me know that I should plan to be a full-time missionary. Since then, I have taken several mission trips to various countries, and my experiences have confirmed my calling. I trust that God will continue to reveal the details of my future.

Furthermore, I have skills in art and writing; and I am majoring in science. At this point, I'm not sure whether these things will fit into God's plan for my life or if these gifts are given to me to use as I wish as I seek to glorify God.

At the moment, I am called to be a college student, a daughter, and a friend. I keep my eyes on the present as well as the future. And as I seek God's will for my life, I remember that my most important calling is to love and obey God through Jesus Christ.

Nicole Jonas, 20 [Indianapolis, Indiana]

[
Take One Step at a Time: Sometimes God does not make our calling obvious. Thomas Merton, a deeply spiritual monk, once said, "You will lead me by the right road, though I may know nothing about it. Therefore I will trust you always though I may seem to be lost."
]

Teach me your way, O LORD,
   and I will walk in your truth.
Psalm 86:11a (NIV)

What's the Plan?

Have you ever leaned back, looked at the stars, and realized how small you are? I have. Yet with all that is going on in the world, God still cares about me, a tiny speck in the midst of a huge universe. God loves me more than I could ever comprehend and put me on this earth for a purpose.

I believe God has a general purpose for all of humanity: We were created to glorify God and to have an intimate relationship with God. I also believe we each have an individual purpose, which God has set out specifically for each of us to accomplish in our lifetime.

So how do we figure out God's individual plan for us? We find our purpose as we grow in relationship with Jesus Christ. In God's own time and in God's own way, the purpose of our life will be revealed. I know it's hard to wait, but I trust that God has some amazing plans for you and me!

Rachel Braz, 18 [Marietta, Georgia]

5-Second Prayer: God, give me patience as your purpose for my life unfolds. Amen.

Part 2

[LISTENING FOR GOD]

WHERE DO I BELONG?

If you struggle to know where you belong, read these devotions, trusting that you belong to and with God. Ask God those questions you keep secret in your heart. Ask God to reveal God's self to you. Ask God where you belong. Then open your heart to hear—and believe—the words of grace and affirmation that God sends. You are unique and uniquely gifted to participate in the transformation of this world with God. Trust in God's love for you and God's wisdom. Hear God speaking directly to you.

As you pray in the coming weeks, simply rest and listen. Turn off your iPod, walk away from the computer, silence your phone, close the door—and listen for God's still, small voice.

God loves you and has chosen you as his own special people. So be gentle, kind, humble, meek, and patient.
Colossians 3:12 (CEV)

Be Yourself

How many times have people told you to be yourself? If you've had the same kinds of experiences I've had, you're sick of hearing it. You would rather be told *how* to be yourself.

I used to be shy. I was so shy that I was scared to talk to people. Over and over, people told me just to be myself. So eventually, I decided to try it. After all, being myself couldn't be that hard, could it?

I discovered that I had to know myself to be myself. Suddenly, the challenge was much more difficult. I didn't know who I was, and I had no idea how to find out. Still, people kept telling me to be myself.

For years, I struggled with figuring myself out. Finally, it occurred to me that I could be whoever I wanted to be; that corny line my parents and kindergarten teacher had told me was true. If I wanted to be loving, spontaneous, caring, I could be. I started thinking of personality traits I wanted to have.

I realized, with considerable amazement, that I already had many of them. I was already on the way to becoming the person I wanted to be!

Rachon Allen, 16 [Vancouver, Washington]

[
Try This: Imagine that you are introducing yourself in the third person. What would you say? Who is the person that God created you to be?
]

Hope does not disappoint us, because God has poured out his love into our hearts by the Holy Spirit, whom he has given us.
Romans 5:5 (NIV)

Grace: God's Greatest Surprise

When God loved me,
when I knew God loved me,
my heart skipped a beat.
I caught my breath
    and let the awesome feelings flow.

I knew I hadn't done a thing
to deserve the kind of love
    God poured out all over me.

I couldn't find the answer
    to Why does God love me?
And now I seldom try.

I just live and breathe and walk
in the radiance of a love
    far beyond my comprehension,
    way beyond my wildest dreams—
grace—a gift God gave
with no strings attached,
    wrapped in the freedom to be me.

And I know no other response
but to simply,
    humbly,
    gratefully,
accept it.

Tanya Ferdinandusz [Colombo, Sri Lanka]

> Journal: Write about a time when you were surprised by God's love.

If you are wise, you are wise for yourself.
Proverbs 9:12a (NRSV)

Self-Conscious

My dad always says, "Find out who you are before you get involved with someone else." That's good advice. I want to be secure enough to be me, to be Annie. I don't want to be known as Tom's girlfriend.

Sometimes we think that we have to be something we're not, that to gain acceptance we have to be cool. But people are accepting. In fact, being cool means knowing who we are and being ourselves.

Someone once asked me to describe myself in two words. I said, "Annie Norris." I know who I am. I am a Christian, an animal lover, a student, a French-horn player, an actor, a singer, a sister, a daughter, a child of God. And I know that God loves and accepts me, even if sometimes it seems that no one else does.

Annie Norris, 20 [Farmington, Maine]

Reflect: Which relationships in your life draw you closer to God, to the heart of God, where you belong? Which ones pull you away? Which relationships do you need to nurture? And which ones might you need to end?

You [God] will call and I will answer you.
Job 14:15a (NIV)

Freedom

Thinking that my senior year of high school would be a cakewalk was as far from the truth as I could get. Nothing is quite like seeing your previous choices and your future decisions come together in a matter of days. It's scary. It's especially scary when all of your friends have awesome plans to go to Christian schools and to serve God in ministry and you feel called to pursue something completely different. God called me to journalism, a field in which I'm told a secular school would provide the best education. After months of struggling, I knew I had to obey my calling. I also realized that going to a secular university would offer me an opportunity for evangelism.

As long as we put our faith in God, we don't need to worry about our future. God will help us to make the right decisions and to find the good in difficult situations. Believe me, trusting God is the most freeing and amazing feeling in the world.

Zack Baldwin, 18 [Schoharie, New York]

[
Think About This: Stress is caused not only by what happens to us but also by our reactions. I have learned that worrying is pointless. If I can change the situation, fine. If I can't, I can make the best of it. Confident, happy people are those who have learned to be content whatever happens. Check out Philippians 4:4-7, 10-13.
]

I recommend having fun, because there is nothing better for people to do in this world than to eat, drink, and enjoy life. That way they will experience some happiness along with all the hard work God gives them.

Ecclesiastes 8:15 (NLT)

Embrace the Possibilities

When I opened my planner, my blood pressure began to rise. Appointments, lists, and reminders filled each week and dictated my life. *Shouldn't there be more to life?* I thought. *What about relaxing? Or seizing the day?*

I knew that I needed to make a change, so I decided to leave one blank line in my planner each day—space for something new and exciting. At first it was difficult to think of things to do, but I soon realized that I didn't need big adventures to spice up my life. Little things—watching butterflies sip nectar from a flower or playing dominoes with my little brother—changed my life in remarkable ways. Instead of dreading each morning, I began to embrace the possibilities of each new day.

Christina Dotson [North Fairfield, Ohio]

Spice It Up

You don't have to be cloistered in a candlelit room to experience God's presence and joy. Try these ideas to seek God's presence in the midst of your busy days:

- Browse through a picture book.
- Tell a family member how much you love him or her.
- Look through photos from your childhood.
- Take a nature walk and talk with God.

The Lord takes delight in his people.
Psalm 149:4a (NIV)

All the World's a Stage

I once was asked, "What do you do for God?" When I responded, "I act," my questioner was surprised and confused.

I love theater. When I step onto a stage and into the story of another human being's life, I experience the presence of God. I feel more connected to the world God created and to the people in it than I ever do in my daily life. So naturally, my dramatic endeavors have become an outlet for praise.

Not everyone loves theater. Not everyone loves basketball. But everyone loves something. When asked about their gifts and talents, many people say, "I don't have any. I just do a lot of things OK." Our gifts do not come as neatly wrapped packages that assure us of success or worldly recognition. Maybe the gift God gives is a passion for something, regardless of our ability to excel. After all, if we could master God's gifts, why would we need the fruit of the Spirit: love, joy, peace, patience, kindness, goodness, faithfulness, gentleness, and self-control (Galatians 5:22-23)?

In the movie *Chariots of Fire*, Eric Liddell declares: "When I run I feel [God's] pleasure." He didn't have to win a gold medal to feel that way, and I don't have to win an Oscar to feel God's pleasure either.

Elisabeth Sweatt, 18 [Asheville, North Carolina]

[**Reflect:** What are your gifts? What are you doing when you "feel God's pleasure"?]

The LORD gives strength to his people;
the LORD blesses his people with peace.

Psalm 29:11 (NIV)

Finding Peace

Books pile high and fill my mind,
    surrounding me on every side.
"Get work done, no time for fun."
    It seems that life keeps piling on.

I've learned it's easier to find
    some peace within my worried mind
when I can stop for just a while—
    letting go of the weighty pile—
to think of Jesus and the promises he made,
    of his great love that will never fade.

Life may be hard; that is true,
    but it's easier to push through
when I bear in mind what Christ has done,
    knowing through him my life is won.

I don't think God meant for me
    to live my life so stressfully;
so the next time this angst hits,
    I'll think of Jesus and the peace he gives.

Ian Kraft, 18 [Burke, Virginia]

Be Reminded: To help me focus on God in the craziness of my life, I carry a small Bible in my backpack. Seeing or touching the Bible when I dig through my bag reminds me that Jesus is with me and is waiting to hear from me. What can you carry with you as a reminder to focus on God during busy days?

Shaun Stevenson, 20 [Aloha, Oregon]

Belonging or Not

For most of my life, I've thought of myself as an outsider. I'm painfully shy, and I have conservative Christian values. Put that all together, and what do you get? Someone who doesn't fit in and who often feels like an outsider.

I'm not a hermit. I'm active in my church; I'm involved in clubs at my college, and I'm always surrounded by lots of people. Still, I don't feel as if I fit in anywhere.

Sometimes I wish I were more outgoing and friendly, but I'm not. Sometimes I am tempted to compromise my Christian values, but I don't. I often rearrange other aspects of my life, hoping to become one of the group; but it doesn't seem to work. I've prayed, asking God to let me feel like I fit in; and God has answered my prayers to some degree. So I'll continue to be who I am; and I'll keep praying until that day when I wake up and say, "Hey, I really do belong here! I'm not an outsider anymore."

Joshua Conway, 22 [Altoona, Pennsylvania]

[**5-Second Prayer:** God, confirm in these moments of silence that I belong to you.]

Love the LORD your God, listen to his voice, and hold fast to him. For the LORD is your life.

Deuteronomy 30:20a (NIV)

The Reason for Living

Over the past year, I've gone from being a faithless person who believed she had no reason to live to being a person who loves life and tries to make the best of every day.

My road to recovery and to God began with one of the worst things a person can do: I attempted suicide—not once, not twice, but three times.

I knew I needed help, so I turned to my friends. One of my best friends suggested that I turn to God for guidance. Every day before school, we prayed together, asking God to help me find my reason for living. I discovered that one of my purposes in life is to listen to others and to help them.

When you wonder, *what's the point?* look to God for answers. God put you on earth for a reason. Search for that reason and live life to its fullest.

Chantel Knight, 19 [New Llano, Louisiana]

[
Prayer: God, help me to find my purpose in life so that, holding fast to your amazing grace, I can live life to its fullest. Amen.
]

Jesus told Simon, "Don't be afraid! From now on you will bring in people instead of fish."
Luke 5:10b (CEV)

Dancing with Purpose

School shootings, concerts turned into riots, drug abuse—are these symptoms of a lack of direction or purpose in life? Our lives need direction, and people who lash out at society seem to have no direction. They're confused and angry, and may not even know why they do such things.

While such confusion makes it hard to hear voices of truth, there is one voice that we must listen to: God's. God tells us that we each have a reason—a purpose—for being. God tells us that we belong, no matter how badly we mess up.

God gives us purpose: to serve God. This does not necessarily mean that we must sell all that we own and go to seminary. It simply means that we must listen for what God has uniquely called and gifted us to do. Just as Jesus invited the disciples to turn their efforts from fish to people, he has a unique invitation and purpose for each of us.

You may not know your purpose now. You may feel as if you're at a crossroads and do not know which direction to take. There is nothing wrong with that. It's an opportunity to seek God's purpose for your life.

Pursue God's purpose for you. God's voice may become clearer through your relationships with others: family, friends, community. God will help you to see the next step.

David Drebes, 17 [Fredericksburg, Virginia]

[**Think About This:** What you are is God's gift to you. What you become is your gift to God.]

PREPARING FOR MY NEW LIFE: BEYOND WHAT I SEE

In this pivotal time in life, it is natural to be consumed with questions about "me" and "my gifts and challenges." But take some time to shift your focus to God, the world, and the needs of God's people. Imagine your focus expanding like a bubble from your own concerns, stresses, and joys to include your family . . . your friends . . . the city where you live . . . your country . . . the world. The entire world is held within the heart of God. Ask God this question: How do you want me to live and work in the midst of this world?

As you pray in the coming weeks about preparing for your new life, remember that you live within a community of people, within tensions and harmony. How can you best prepare yourself for the realities and the hopes of the world?

Moses said to the LORD, . . . "I am slow of speech and slow of tongue." Then the LORD said to him, "Who gives speech to mortals? . . . Is it not I, the LORD? Now go, and I will be with your mouth."

Exodus 4:10b-12 (NRSV)

God Calling?

Your calling is a lot bigger than just your job. God asks us to give our entire lives over to God's call to us.

You get a hunch, a feeling, a nudge. You sense that you are supposed to use your gifts and talents in a certain way. Sometimes you hear people say nice things about you and wonder if they mean something bigger—things such as, "You sure are kind to others." Or, "I've never seen anyone draw or paint as well as you do." Or, "It's amazing how you ace those math and science tests!" A thought about the future, a good feeling about a skill, a friend's praise—could God be starting to call you to your life's vocation?

The words *vocation* and *vocalizing* are similar. They both have to do with a voice making a sound. When God's voice calls someone to his or her life's work, that work is his or her vocation. Another word for vocation is *calling*. God uniquely calls each person.

Most likely, your call will not come all at once. By listening to God's voice through the voices of people you love and trust and by listening to the voice within, you will someday know what you are to do with your life. You will gain confidence about your calling and launch into your life's work. But how will you know what's right for you?

Test the Call

You probably have already begun to use your gifts and talents in small, maybe short-term, ways. Susan might use her artistic skills to create greeting cards for persons who are homebound. Dylan, who has a good speaking voice, might agree to read scripture in worship. Karen may use her organizational skills to start a student group against drunk driving. A life's vocation is a larger version of these little calls.

Listen to feedback from others who know you. Then ask them for insights if you feel pulled in a certain direction. Thinking about teaching? Speak to a teacher. Considering preaching? Visit your pastor. The first way to test your call is to try it out in small ways. For example, if you enjoy writing, try writing for **devozine**. (Visit www.devozine.org for complete writers' guidelines and themes of upcoming issues.)

A Leap of Faith

Some vocations require more education after high school, so as you gather information about colleges, universities, or trade schools, you will sense if this direction is right for you. Committing to a school or to a direction in higher education is a leap of faith, a further way to test your call. And then, as you take classes and perhaps feel called to change your training or course of study, this may be a way that God leads you in a new direction.

It's About Becoming You

When Paul wrote to the church at Corinth, he knew the importance of each person trusting his or her unique call.

No one's call was better or worse than anyone else's. First Corinthians 12:4-6 is a wonderful passage to remember when you might be heading in a different direction than some of your friends are.

There are varieties of calls and ways to be called. Moses was called through a voice in a burning bush. Isaiah felt his mouth touched. Jesus' mother, Mary, saw an angel.

Remember that the work to which you will be called will be a lot bigger than just your job, because God asks us to give our entire lives over to God's call to us.

A Really Fun Journey

Sorting out your future and listening for God's leading might seem a little scary. What about this do you fear? What about this seems cool and even exciting? Learning more about who you are and about where you might be headed can be fun! Just give yourself lots of time and lots of conversation with others; and remember that God is always with you.

Robert Roth [East Lansing, Michigan]

> Reflect: Jesus was called through his baptism and got a clear sense of what he was to do: "He has sent me to proclaim release to the captives and recovery of sight to the blind, to let the oppressed go free, to proclaim the year of the Lord's favor" (Luke 4:18b-19, NRSV).
>
> What events in your life have to do with your potential calling? What have you learned about your potential calling through these events?

Wondering

Who am I?
Lord, why don't I know?

I look at the stars
    dotting the midnight sky.
I am so insignificant.

I stand in the wash of a roaring ocean,
    waves crashing before me.
I am so weak.

I look to the mountains,
    majestic and beautiful.
I am so unworthy.

Who am I, Lord?
Who am I really?

I am your creation,
    a masterpiece of your hand.
I am your child.

Kristen Torres-Toro, 16 [Jonesboro, Georgia]

[
    Try This: Draw a picture of the universe. Include the
    galaxies, planets, and stars. Draw God in the picture.
    Draw yourself. How does this picture give you a
    different perspective on your questions and concerns?
]

For this gospel I was appointed a herald and an apostle and
a teacher. . . . But I am not ashamed, for I know the one in
whom I have put my trust.

2 Timothy 1:11-12a (NRSV)

Called

Over the past few years, I have been a member of the
Nazarene Bible Quizzing League and have been able to do
in-depth studies of Luke, John, and a few of Paul's letters.
At first it seemed to me that both Jesus and Paul sounded
high-and-mighty. But as I continued my studies, I realized
instead that Jesus and Paul were absolutely sure of who they
were and of what God had called them to do. They spoke
with confidence.

Then it hit me: God has called me to do something
special in my life too. I don't have to be shy or conservative
about God's call or pretend that I'm someone I'm not. Jesus
and Paul were both humble people, but they were also
sure of who they were. Self-consciousness did not stand in
their way.

Kelsey Nichols, 17 [Matthews, North Carolina]

[
Personalize Scripture: Rewrite and pray 2 Timothy
1:11-12a to reflect a situation where you need
confidence. For what tasks have you been appointed?
How does your faith bring new confidence?
]

> Then you will have success if you are careful to observe the decrees and laws that the LORD gave Moses for Israel. Be strong and courageous. Do not be afraid or discouraged.
>
> **1 Chronicles 22:13 (NIV)**

Consider These Seven Secrets of Success

How many of the following traits or habits do you already have? Ask God to help you incorporate one of the "secrets" into your life, and see what happens.

S ingle-minded devotion to God
U ncompromising obedience to God
C ommitment to people
C ommitment to tasks
E ndurance for the long haul
S earching the scriptures
S pending time in prayer

Tanya Ferdinandusz [Colombo, Sri Lanka]

Think About It: Success is waking up in the morning, whoever you are, wherever you are, however old or young, and bounding out of bed because there's something out there that you love to do, that you believe in, that you're good at, something that's bigger than you are, and you can hardly wait to get at it again today.

—Whit Hobbs

A friend loves at all times.
Proverbs 17:17a (NIV)

There for Me

Lately, my life has been hard. My parents are getting divorced, I'm going to college, and I'm having a lot of new experiences. I don't know what I would have done without my two best friends, Jessica and Suzanna. In the last eight years, they have always been there for me. They would do anything for me, and they stand by me through the bad times. They are also there when I'm happy or excited.

Friends like Jessica and Suzanna are hard to find. Proverbs 17:17 says that "a friend loves at all times," but we have so few friends who do just that. When such a friend comes into our lives, we cherish him or her, knowing that friendship is a gift from God. I am grateful to God that I have found such good friends.

Amelia Rollings, 19 [Columbia, South Carolina]

[**Reflect:** In what ways do you show your friends that you love them at all times? How can you be a better friend this week?]

Cast all your anxiety on [God] because he cares for you.
1 Peter 5:7 (NIV)

Worrywart

I must admit that I am a worrywart. I worry about the big test coming up or how my school pictures will turn out. I worry about how I'll perform in a concert or a basketball game. I worry a lot about passing the test for my driver's license. And just thinking about going to college or getting a job sends me into a cold sweat.

It helps to remember that I can take my worries to God and that God will give me the strength and wisdom to handle them. Scripture reminds me that I shouldn't lose sleep over my uncertainties and fears because God cares for me. God will lead me through all the obstacles life throws my way. Of course, I still have to study for the test and practice for the concert; but I'm learning that agonizing over them won't help. So the next time I start fretting about the big game or a crucial decision, I'll say a prayer and let God take over.

Evan Hall, 17 [Luck, Wisconsin]

Something to Remember: My sister Victoria taught me that God is in control. God has given Victoria an incredible outlook on life. She bases everything she does on the idea that God is in control—or GIC, as I now abbreviate it. If we simply let go of our worry, we can sit back and watch God's amazing, unfolding plan.

Javed Sommers, 18 [Alberta, Canada]

Give me again the joy that comes from your salvation,
and make me willing to obey you.

Psalm 51:12 (GNT)

How I Long

Oh, how I need him
    to fill me with his presence,
    to change me from within!
But to ask for help—
    I wouldn't know where to begin.
For too long, my life has revolved around sin;
    for too long, I've loved hate instead of compassion.
How I long to feel genuine joy,
    to be happy inside,
    to start caring whether I live or die,
    to be able to cry, to stop living this lie!
How I long to be able to help,
    to feel the way I once felt,
    to have Christ in my life,
    to talk with him every night!
I want so badly to get down on my knees
    and beg God's forgiveness,
to ask God to give me a new heart,
    so my only concern would be to please God.
How I long to be able to tell sin to flee,
    so my life would be only Jesus and me!

Cody Howell, 21 [Lake City, Florida]

Ask—God Will Change Your Heart

You bring beauty to my life
    even when I am fallen,
      dying from lack of faith.
You color me with shades of grace
    and infuse me with hope.
There is no depth to which I drop
    where you cannot find me
      and redeem me with your love.
By living for you, I die to myself
    and discover the colors
      you painted in my soul.

Melinda Williams [Box Elder, South Dakota]

> Speaking the truth in love, we will in all things grow up into him who is the Head, that is, Christ.
> **Ephesians 4:15 (NIV)**

It's OK to Question

I love my church because it's the place where I can voice questions, even doubts, about my Christian faith. My church is friendly to people in all stages of their faith journey, even those who haven't made a commitment to Christ.

I don't think all churches are like mine. Some believers feel that questioning can compromise the integrity of their faith. When someone expresses an opinion contrary to their own, they want to set the person straight. In clinging so tightly to one set of ideals and one understanding of scripture, I wonder if we are closing the door to God's truth.

I've been a Christian for twenty years, and I feel most free to be me when I can voice my questions and opinions without fear of immediate judgment. How hard it must be for those at the beginning of their Christian walk who don't have a safe place to ask questions and to explore their faith. Because I want others to feel free and comfortable around me, I look for opportunities to embrace loving discussion.

Faydra Stratton [Wilmington, North Carolina]

[
Reflect: With whom do you feel free to express your opinions and to talk about your beliefs? What can you do to help other people speak freely?
]

Jesus said, "Prophets are honored by everyone, except the people of their hometown and . . . their own family."
Mark 6:4 (CEV)

Faith of My Own

As we get older, we move farther and farther from the nest of our parents' household. We start driving; we push to extend our curfew; we leave home for college or a career. During the process of redefining ourselves as individuals, many of us find Christ for the first time or in a deeper way.

If your parents don't share your faith, talking with them about the changes in your life can be difficult. They may not understand, or they may not believe that you know something they don't know.

How can you keep your faith strong? How can you share your faith with your parents?

- Pray. Remember what led you to Christ.
- Talk with your parents about your faith and offer to answer their questions.
- Let them see Christ in the way you live.
- Stay involved in a small group that supports you.
- Ask your parents to accept your faith as a decision you have made as an adult and will stick to for life.

Stefanie Peters, 20 [The Woodlands, Texas]

Reflect: How has your faith changed as you have matured? How have you made your faith your own?

When You Can't Kiss It Better

There are some things a kiss can't fix. Circumstances in our lives change without warning, sometimes for the worse. Sadness is part of life, and even Christians are hit hard.

At those times, we try to remember that God loves us unconditionally. God knows our hearts and minds. Does this mean we don't need to talk to God? No, we need to pray and to express our sadness. Whenever I've done this, I've felt a huge weight lifted from my shoulders.

Instead of saying quick prayers or simply listing all of our requests, why don't we open up and tell God how we really feel? God desires a relationship with us, and God has big shoulders to cry on.

Stephen Kolibaba, 17 [Portland, Oregon]

[Just a Thought
> To Mercy, Pity, Peace, and Love
> All pray in their distress.
>
> —William Blake
]

I have learned to be content whatever the circumstances.
Philippians 4:11b (NIV)

Count Your Blessings

Years ago, a friend told me the key to happiness is learning to be thankful for what you have. She challenged me to find one thing every day I am thankful for. I started writing in a notebook a sentence or two about the good things that happened each day. Even on bad days, I did not succumb to the temptation to write about anything negative. I began to see that no matter how difficult my life seemed, I could always find something to be glad about.

I started this project a year before I became a Christian, and I love seeing how my thoughts have been transformed since then. I have learned that whatever circumstances life may throw at me, I am able to write that Jesus loves me, and I love Jesus—and that makes every day wonderful.

Nicole Jonas, 23 [Indianapolis, Indiana]

Keep a Book of Thanks. Every day, write down one thing you are thankful for. Some people use a calendar. I keep my thanks in a journal. This poem is on the first page:

I'm writing here my book of thanks,
small things that fill each day.
I'm writing them so you will know
what my heart wants to say.
When I write each little thanks,
they seem to multiply.
The Lord sends blessings every day.
There is no short supply.

Carolyn Caines [Kelso, Washington]

DECISION MAKING

It's tempting to think that life after high school will be radically different from the last twelve years. You are finally a young adult—surely you will act more mature and make better decisions. Your relationships will be stronger. The classes you take will serve a purpose. New freedoms will make life better.

But the truth is that, even as you move into the future, you will cover some of the same ground. You will find yourself in similar circumstances with friends, boyfriends or girlfriends, schoolwork, and jobs. You may view them differently now, however—in the light of your changing relationship with God and the experience you have gained over the years.

As you continue in your devotions, begin to see your life and your spiritual journey through the eyes of God.

God is patient, because he wants everyone to turn from sin and no one to be lost.

2 Peter 3:9b (CEV)

God Waits for Us

How patiently you wait
    for me to see you,
    to look
        beyond the distractions
            that color my world
        and realize your presence,
    to filter
        through the noise of living,
    to hear
        your still, soft voice.

How patiently you wait
    for me to see
    where you have
        confirmed your love,
        consecrated my life,
        made each moment holy.

How patiently you wait
    for me
        without ever giving up.

Melinda Williams [Box Elder, South Dakota]

Look and See: When have you realized that God had been waiting patiently for you to make a decision? How did it feel to finally recognize God's voice? to feel God's presence? to know God's unfailing love?

"For who has known the mind of the Lord that he may instruct him?" But we have the mind of Christ.
1 Corinthians 2:16 (NIV)

The Mind of Christ

My days are full of running around—to school, to softball practice, then home, and to a million other places. It's no surprise, then, that when I take time each night to examine my day, I find many situations in which I didn't have "the mind of Christ."

Every morning, I pray about the day and ask God to use me as God sees fit; but the next time I talk to God is usually before I go to bed. I need to have the mind of Christ throughout the day, when I'm taking a quiz or standing in the lunch line, when I'm stretching for softball practice, and when I'm driving to and from church.

The only way to keep the mind of Christ is to be in constant communication with Christ: to pray continually and to read and study God's Word. When we are in tune with Christ, when he is close to our hearts, then we can have the mind of Christ. And it will show in everything we do, from simple daily activities to major decisions. If we seek to walk with Christ throughout each day, no matter what happens, we can face it with the mind of Christ.

Christy Lee, 18 [Winston-Salem, North Carolina]

Change Your "Mind": Choose one day in the next week to focus on God's presence. Awake with a prayer. Talk to God about each thing that happens—good or bad. Try to be like Christ to those you meet. Close your day by examining what went well and what was difficult. Fall asleep giving thanks to God for everything.

Choosing to Be Me

After every choice I make, I find out more about myself.

So far I have discovered a lot about who I am not. I am not my grades. I am not my place of employment. I am not my clothes. (I ignore the saying "The clothes make the person"; they don't.) I am not the car I drive. I am not my lunch (a cheeseburger). I am not what other people think of me. I am not my race or my religion.

So what have I learned about who I am? I am my values and my morals. I am my thoughts and my feelings. I am my opinions. I am a child of God.

I have not found out everything about who I am, but I discover a little more with every choice I make.

Andrew Shipka, 22 [Youngstown, Ohio]

[
Act on It: The next time you have a choice to make, ask yourself: What will my choice say about who I am? Am I comfortable with how my choice will affect other people?
]

> What does the LORD your God require of you? Only to fear the LORD your God, to walk in all his ways, to love him, to serve the LORD your God with all your heart and with all your soul.
> **Deuteronomy 10:12 (NRSV)**

God's Expectations

We often think that our parents set standards too high for us or put too much pressure on us to succeed. But we also set expectations for ourselves. Our parents hope and pray for us. They offer advice. Sometimes they push. And sometimes we push ourselves. But we choose the standards that we think we can reach.

We are often critical and unsure of ourselves, so we try to be like other people. We do what they do and try to live up to their expectations, even if their choices are not the right choices.

When I'm unsure of myself, I try to follow God's direction and try to live according to God's expectations. I've learned that even when I don't know what to do, I can trust God to lead me.

Jessica Andersen, 18 [Pine River, Wisconsin]

Reflect: As you move into the future, where do you need to trust God to lead you?

> [Jesus said,] "If any want to become my followers, let them deny themselves and take up their cross and follow me."
> **Mark 8:34b (NRSV)**

Take Up Your Cross

"What are you planning to do after college?" This question is frequently sprung upon me, and it never fails to trigger a surge of panic. *What am I going to do with my life?* I wonder. *What does God want me to do? Am I cut out to be a teacher? writer? psychologist?*

Jesus calls us to deny ourselves, to take up our cross, and to follow him. The cross meant death for Jesus in order to secure our salvation, but it also represents God's plan for our lives. We carry out God's plan by choosing to do God's will and by using the gifts God has given us to serve others.

Though I may feel lost in a sea of choices, I have plenty of time to discover my calling. Until then, I can strive to do God's will each day and keep praying that God will guide me—and give me patience.

Evan Hall, 20 [Luck, Wisconsin]

How Do You Discern God's Will?
Before I make a choice, I see whether the Bible addresses the topic; and if it does, I try to be obedient. I pray about my dilemma and ask for other people's opinions. Then I make a decision. I believe that if we are following God's commands, the choices we make will line up with God's plan. Plus, God wants us to use our minds. If life were all mapped out for us, it wouldn't be as much of an adventure.

Karen Earls [Ontario, Canada]

[Jesus said,] "I have come in order that you might have life—
life in all its fullness."
John 10:10b (GNT)

It's My Life

I have a life.
It may not be as exciting as yours,
    but it's my life.
        I make my own choices.

I have a life.
I may not go out as often as you,
    but it's my life.
        I think my own thoughts.

I have a life.
I may not have as many friends as you,
    but I'm my own person—
        and my future is full of possibilities.

Jan Jones [Nevada City, California]

Journal: How do you live your life? Do you think your
choices please God?

In six days the LORD made heaven and earth, the sea, and all
that is in them, but rested the seventh day; therefore the Lord
blessed the sabbath day and consecrated it.
Exodus 20:11 (NRSV)

Throwing Away the Lists

Eventually, I get to a point, near the end of a semester, when
lists take over my life. I become incapable of focusing on
what I am currently doing. All I can see are my reminders
of what still needs to get done. I realize that I need to do
some things that are fun, so I add them to my list. Then, of
course, they are no longer fun; they are simply a few more
things to do on an already long list. At that point, when all
my days are swallowed up in planned activities that contain
no joy, I realize it's time to throw the lists—all of them—into
the trash.

I remind myself of how lucky I am. I am lucky to be in
graduate school, reading books I want to read and writing
papers about art, which I love. I am grateful to have a job as
a tutor, to help people learn how to read and to go home
feeling good about myself. I thank God for good friends
who care about me and who make me laugh even when
I'm stressed.

Why should I treat my friends, my job, and my
schoolwork as chores? Why should I drag my feet and dread
the deadlines when I could simply enjoy the life that I have
chosen and the gifts that God has given me?

Throwing away my lists is hard to do. Breaking free from my mapped-out mental state is even harder. But it's worth trying. It's worth completely immersing myself in my homework or running around town with my friends without a thought for what I have to do next. It's worth trying to enjoy life because life is a celebration!

Rachel Crumpler [Astoria, New York]

> **Try This:** Make a to-do list for the week; then throw it away. Set aside three hours this weekend to do something you want to do—or do nothing at all. Enjoy every second of it. Thank God for your life.

[Jesus said,] "If you are tired from carrying heavy burdens, come to me and I will give you rest."
Matthew 11:28 (CEV)

Soul Pressure

Pressure
I feel it
    surrounding my soul
    taunting me
    prodding me
        to give in to temptation
        to fall to the enemy
        to sin.

Pressure
I feel it
    pushing from all sides,
    driving me,
    forcing me
        to go deeper within
        to retreat from the world
        to seek my God,
            my only escape.

Pressure
I feel it.

Casey Colombo, 20 [Kingsport, Tennessee]

[**Reflect:** How do you deal with the pressure to give in to temptation? Where do you seek and find God?]

Off the Roller Coaster

You know the problem with roller coasters: once they start, you can't get off until they stop, no matter how sick you get. Have you ever felt sick about life? Have you wanted to get off the ride?

The good thing about roller coasters is that they can be fun. I used to hate roller coasters. Now I'm the guy in the front seat, screaming my head off.

My life has had its ups and downs. There was a time when I thought life would work out for some people but not for me. I was miserable. I wanted out, and I tried to escape. I closed people off. I used drugs. I rebelled. I tried my best to check out.

How About You?

The following list shows some of the ways people run away. Mark the ones you've considered:

- avoiding people
- using drugs
- rebelling
- pretending to be someone you're not
- putting down or bullying other people
- refusing to accept responsibility
- choosing abusive relationships and staying in them
- being overly negative
- having sex
- drinking

- watching pornography
- playing violent video games
- listening to negative or violent music
- engaging in violent behavior
- being apathetic
- hurting yourself or other people

The Secret of Riding Life's Roller Coasters

So how do we learn to live life to the fullest? Remember these secrets to riding life's roller coasters:

R ely on God.

O bstacles are challenges, not problems.

L ive life abundantly.

L ove, even though you might get hurt.

E njoy what you have.

R esist escaping.

C reate more positive ways of approaching life.

O pportunities will present themselves when you look for them.

A ccept yourself.

S mile more often.

T ake time to work through problems.

E scape negative relationships, behavior, and attitudes.

R each out for help.

S cared? Put your arms in the air and scream to God!

Life is an adventure. Explore and enjoy the world God has created for you.

When to Escape

There are times when we need to run. Escaping isn't always bad. In fact, the Bible commands us to flee from certain situations; check out 1 Timothy 6:9-11 and 2 Timothy 2:22. You should escape from abusive relationships, temptation, evil—anything that comes between you and God.

Warning! When the Bible tells us to flee, it doesn't stop there. When we run away, we should run to God. We flee from evil, and we pursue God! Now that's a good place to be.

Jim Still-Pepper [Zanesville, Ohio]

> Think About It: Read aloud John 10:10. Then read it again. Think about what this verse means for your life. Jesus wants you to enjoy life, to live life to the fullest. The ride of your life awaits you! Climb on!

The Search
(Written for a friend who doesn't know God)

Head in your hands
you sit there,
reflecting on your life,
on the brink of despair.

Friend, this is not
the way it's supposed to be.
There is more to life
if you believe.

Keep trying, keep seeking;
You'll find what you're needing.
I'll help you, be with you.
Don't give up hope; you can't lose.
A better life awaits you.
Never give up the search.

Love, please don't forget,
will carry you through.
When you need a friend,
I will never leave you.

Keep trying, keep seeking;
You'll find what you're needing.
I'll help you, be with you.
Don't give up hope; you can't lose.
A better life awaits you.
Never give up the search.

Nicole Jonas, 24 [Indianapolis, Indiana]

> **Reflect:** When have you made a decision to keep trying, to keep seeking? Tell God what you need today.

Part 3

[COMING TOGETHER]

NEW FRIENDS

We don't walk this journey of faith alone. We walk with friends, relying on one another for prayer, laughter, wisdom, and support.

As you use the devotions, think about friends you have met along your journey. Pray for those you have yet to meet.

Jonathan became one in spirit with David, and he loved him as himself.

1 Samuel 18:1b (NIV)

One in Spirit

One Sunday when I was in college, I went to church alone. I hadn't been there for weeks and was struggling with spiritual questions. I went to church looking not for answers but for a sign that I wasn't alone.

I slipped into the pew next to a guy who looked about my age; and after the service, we introduced ourselves. Later we went to a coffee shop, where we had an animated theological argument that quickly progressed into a deep spiritual discussion. It was the first time he had been to church in a long time too; and we discovered that we shared similar struggles, hopes, and fears.

He has remained one of my closest friends. We still argue over theology, moral questions, and politics; but he encourages me to grow in faith. I feel quite comfortable asking him to pray for me. I can ask him, "How is it with your soul?" and get an honest answer. My friend has also taught me to pray the Liturgy of the Hours, an ancient form of prayer that involves meditating on the scriptures at different times of the day. I treasure God's gift of my friend in faith.

Joanna Hubbard Shindler, 24 [Lawton, Oklahoma]

> **Reflect:** What does it mean to be one in spirit? How can friends encourage each other to grow even when they disagree?

Some friends play at friendship
but a true friend sticks closer than one's nearest kin.
Proverbs 18:24 (NRSV)

The Miracle of Friendship

A true friend, a friend who always understands, is a miracle. Sometimes my friend Kelly knows what I'm thinking without my saying a word.

I'm no artist—I consider stick figures challenging—but I needed a fine arts credit to graduate from college. I was working on my art project; and the more I worked, the worse it got. Finally I gave up. I knew I would fail the class and miss graduation. I tried to keep my fears to myself, but Kelly knew. She stopped by my room the night before the project was due, took one look at my face, and knew.

"I'm never going to finish this!" I burst into tears. "I can't do it."

"Yes, you can," she said immediately. "You can do anything."

Just like that, she made me feel better. She spent the rest of the evening helping me measure, cut, and glue Popsicle sticks until the project was finished—lopsided but finished.

I appreciated her help; but more important was her belief in me, which gave me strength when I needed it. In a single moment, she showed me the power of faith. There's something miraculous about a friend like Kelly!

Kimberly Haugh [Chesterfield, Missouri]

[Take Action: Think of a friend who sticks closer to you than your nearest kin. Write a letter of thanks to him or her.]

It is the LORD who goes before you. He will be with you; he will not fail you or forsake you. Do not fear or be dismayed.
Deuteronomy 31:8 (NRSV)

Filling the Void

In school, I look around at all the broken lives and ask, "Where are you, God?" I see so many people with shattered lives and with nowhere to turn. They are all searching for something to take away the pain and to fill the void in their lives. They turn to violence, drugs, alcohol, cutting, boyfriends or girlfriends, cursing, sex; but nothing seems to help.

It's easy to blame God for not helping these people. But if I think about it, I realize that all of us are broken. Only through Christ have I found healing and purpose. And God calls me to be an ambassador for Christ, to spread this message of healing and hope.

Deuteronomy 31:8 promises that God is with us, that we never have to be afraid or discouraged. This verse gives me the courage to tell others in my generation that the only way to fill the void in their lives is with the love and peace of Jesus Christ.

Lauren Gossler, 17 [Morgantown, Pennsylvania]

Pray with Scripture: Pray Ephesians 3:17-19 (GNT) for friends who are searching for meaning: (*Name*), "I pray that Christ will make his home in your [heart] through faith. I pray that you may have your roots and foundation in love, so that you, . . . may have the power to understand how broad and long, how high and deep, is Christ's love. Yes, may you come to know his love. . . and so be completely filled with the very nature of God." Amen.

We praise you, Lord God!
You treat us with kindness day after day,
   and you rescue us.
Psalm 68:19 (CEV)

A Little Help, a Little Hope

There have been times when I have been so overwhelmed with work that I felt like screaming. One time in college, I had three term papers all due on the same day. With my regular classwork and a part-time job, I put off writing the papers until the last minute.

I had done the research for all three papers and had made notes, but I had only one paper done the night before they were due. I was close to the breaking point when my friend Nette rescued me.

I had a little refrigerator in my dorm room, but it was empty, and the plug was broken. I wasn't about to take time off to go to the cafeteria, so I had skipped lunch and dinner. Nette came to my door with fast food. She'd bought a new plug for the refrigerator, and she fixed it while I ate. Then she started typing. As I completed each page, she typed it; and I was able to turn in all three papers on time.

When my friend started typing my papers, she gave me more than help; she gave me hope. If she hadn't shown up, I might have given up on completing my assignments. Nette rescued me, and she let me know that I didn't have to deal with my problems alone.

Gina Lee [Burbank, California]

5-Second Prayer: Thank you, God, for people who give us hope. Amen.

> Two are better than one. . . . For if they fall,
> one will lift up the other.
>
> **Ecclesiastes 4:9-10a (NRSV)**

Accountable

Caroline lived two doors down from me during my freshman year of college. We immediately became friends and often hung out together. Soon the leaders of the Christian fellowship we attended encouraged everyone to find an accountability partner—someone we could trust and could talk to honestly about our lives and faith. Caroline and I decided to become partners.

We met once a week to catch up, to celebrate joys, and to talk about faith questions and struggles we were facing. I cherished those times together and the ways we encouraged each other. Our senior year, when a situation arose that I found unfair, Caroline helped me to see the good that had come out of it. We didn't always have answers or solutions, but we were able to listen to and pray for each other.

As a Christian, I want to be a positive example for others; but sometimes I just don't feel very positive. With Caroline, I could be open and honest; I didn't have to worry about projecting a "perfect" image. We grew close because we allowed each other to see our weaknesses and faults as well as our strengths.

Laura Luder, 23 [Swarthmore, Pennsylvania]

[
Act on It: Ask someone you trust to be your accountability partner. Set a time to meet and share joys and concerns. Be yourself. Opening up will deepen your faith and your friendship.
]

The task is too heavy for you; you cannot do it alone.
Exodus 18:18b (NRSV)

Overload

During my sophomore year of college, I led a small group of girls at church, volunteered at a ministry center, went on a mission trip to Honduras, worked on a committee at school, and took a full load of classes. I hadn't planned to do so much, but I never said no when anyone would ask. Before long, I was in over my head—exhausted, crunched for time, and stressed out.

One day, my roommate, Jessica, pulled me aside and said, "I never see you, and I worry about you being stressed all the time. You don't have to push yourself so hard. Nobody expects you to do it all."

Through Jessica, God was gently reminding me that I didn't have to do everything. As I let go of some of the activities in my life, I was able to grow closer to God. I learned that it was OK to say no to some things so that I could say yes to God.

Ann Swindell, 23 [Wheaton, Illinois]

Reflect: God doesn't ask us to handle everything on our own; that's why we have one another. A friend of mine once offered to help me during a stressful time, and I realized I hadn't even thought to ask her.

I was so busy trying to do it all myself that I ignored one of the people God had placed in my life to support and encourage me. Who is waiting to help you if you would only ask?

Kate Traub [Sycamore, Illinois]

Loving Others

When Cassie called at three o'clock in the morning and asked me to pick her up, I was quite annoyed. I was a freshman in college and needed sleep before my journalism final in the morning. But as I listened to her, I could tell that she was crying, upset, and scared. She had gone home with some guys after a party and was stranded. I rolled out of bed, tired and still annoyed, and went to pick her up. We stopped at a 24-hour diner to talk. As I listened to her story, I reconsidered my attitude. Cassie was failing her classes, felt stuck in a bad relationship, and hated herself. I offered her comfort, realizing now that I would not trade this opportunity to help her for anything.

Although I am still passionate about becoming a journalist, Cassie's early morning call reminded me that I need to be passionate about people every day. First John 3:16-18 says that if we see brothers or sisters in need, we ought to help them. That's true love, and helping others in the name of Christ should be our true passion.

Melissa Hart [Champlin, Minnesota]

Think About This: You never know how far a little kindness may go. There are so many people who are unaware of God's love or who are in circumstances that make their lives difficult. If everyone showed God's amazing love to those around them, what an incredible world this would be!

Jessica Green, 17 [Victoria, Australia]

> So then, just as you received Christ Jesus as Lord, continue to live in him, rooted and built up in him, strengthened in the faith as you were taught, and overflowing with thankfulness.
> **Colossians 2:6–7 (NIV)**

The Way I Was, the Way I Am

The way I was before Christ touched my life:
Full of pain and hate,
not caring about anyone—
    no one at all—
my heart was cold.

The day I felt him touch me,
I knew I was changing.

I saw the world,
    cold and dark.
I had done so much wrong;
and every step I took,
    I remembered.
But I have to focus on the present,
    not the past,
because I know what's done is done
    and I cannot change it.

The day I felt him touch me,
I knew I was changing.

I see things differently.
My heart's full of love.

The world is brighter
    loving everyone,
    having a new life.
Now he holds me tight
    and never lets me go
    back to the way I was.

Derek Durigon, 17 [Latrobe, Pennsylvania]

Reflect on God's Amazing Love
Lord, your love is
    so vast and deep,
    I ponder as
    I drift off to sleep.
You tenderly number
    every hair on my head
    and patiently bottle
    each tear that I shed.
You knew me long
    before your presence
    I craved.
And on your hands
    my name is engraved.

Sharon Dyer [Wyoming, Michigan]

INDEPENDENCE DAYS

You began these devotions as a recent graduate. Now you are much closer to independence and a new adventure. Whether you have physically moved out of your home or are simply trying to find your own adult voice and direction, you can be confident that you are moving. Whether you move forward with exhilaration or fear, joy or anxiety, or certainty or doubt, keep moving.

Take the next steps in your devotional life, conscious of your ability to make your own decisions and confident in your new independence alongside God.

Each day brings its own surprises.
Proverbs 27:1b (CEV)

Carpe Diem!

"I'm sick of high school," my sister sighed. "I want to be in college now." I had just started college. After I told my sister what it was like, she didn't want to wait.

I smiled; I had felt the same way in high school. I couldn't wait to be free and to live on my own. Once I got to college, though, I realized that independence comes with huge responsibilities. Suddenly I was busier than ever before, and everyone I talked to said that it would only get worse. I found myself hoping that college would go by quickly so that I would be out of school forever. Talk about freedom!

That's when I caught myself. I was doing exactly what my sister was doing. I wasn't happy with the independence I had. I couldn't make college go by any faster. As long as I was dreaming about the future and wishing to be somewhere else, I couldn't enjoy where I was in the present; so I decided to enjoy the freedom I had, even if it didn't always feel like enough.

Since then I've been having a great time in college, and I'm starting to get used to the added responsibilities. After I stopped looking ahead and started to focus on where I was, college has been everything I dreamed it would be.

John Mark Miller, 19 [Mesquite, Texas]

Try This: Write on a sheet of paper the words *Carpe diem!* Then draw pictures or designs to make a poster for your room. *Carpe diem!* means "Seize the day!" When you see the poster, remember to live each day to the fullest.

Reflecting God's Love

God has called each one of us to show God's love by how we live. However, each of us lives in a different "world," and it's no accident that we are where we are. God has placed us where we are needed most in order to show God's love to others.

But how are we to reflect this love in the world in which we live? Each of us is unique, and we will show God's love in different ways. But first, we need to do two things:

1. **Seek God.** When we realize that we are incapable of doing anything alone, we begin to understand our need for God. As we seek God, we will find God. As we find God, we will love God more and more. We'll become so full of God's love that we can't help but let that love spill out of us for others to see!

2. **Surrender all.** We need to surrender everything to God: our wills, our minds, our lives, and everything in them. When we let God reign in our lives, God will work through us for God's glory. We don't need to worry about how we will reflect God's love; God will take care of that.

Love others by loving God first—it's our call!

Nicki Figley, 16 [East Palestine, Ohio]

[
Reflect: What have you felt God calling you to do with your new independence that would reflect God's love to those around you? How have you responded?
]

[Jesus said,] "As you sent me into the world, I have sent them [my disciples] into the world."
John 17:18 (NIV)

Jesus' Leadership

From Jesus' example of what a leader should be, I have learned these three things:

1. Throughout his ministry, Jesus retreated from the crowds and spent time with God. If I want to be an effective leader and not get burned out, I must regularly spend time alone with God, praying and studying God's Word.

2. Jesus didn't minister by himself; he trained the twelve disciples to minister with him. Matthew 10 tells how Jesus sent the disciples out to do ministry. Because the disciples were trained in ministry, Christianity was able to grow rapidly after Jesus ascended into heaven. As a leader, I can't do everything myself. I must train people to work with me.

3. A leader must reach out to people whom no one else is concerned about. Throughout his ministry, Jesus talked with prostitutes, lepers, Samaritans, and other outcasts of society. He didn't spend his time only with people who were rich, popular, and good-looking. As a leader, I should be willing to reach out to people who are laughed at and are lonely.

You may never hear these points stressed in a leadership training course, but I can't think of a better example of leadership than the life and ministry of Christ!

Joel Newton, 22 [Upland, Indiana]

[**5-Second Prayer:** God, make me the kind of leader that Jesus was. Amen.]

Let me alone, that I may find a little comfort.
Job 10:20b (NRSV)

Go Away!

Don't talk to me.
Leave me alone.
Go do your own thing.

Don't try to tell me you're right.
You're letting others tell you what to do,
    letting others make your decisions,
    taking unwanted advice,
    making choices without thinking about my feelings.

Why don't you understand?
I don't want to live your life.
I have different eyes to see my world,
    a different mouth to speak my opinions,
    a different mind to choose my life.

Maybe I would listen.
Maybe you would understand how I feel
    if you'd let me do what I think is right,
    if you'd let me make my own mistakes, not yours.

Listen to me when I say, "Go away!"

Deidra Smits, 18 [Sterling Heights, Michigan]

[
Journal: Write a letter to God, honestly telling God how
you feel about becoming more independent. Know that
God understands if you need to use strong words.
]

Success, success to you,
and success to those who help you,
for your God will help you.

1 Chronicles 12:18b (NIV)

Accepting God's Help

I am a strong-willed person. I love my freedom. I am determined, and I truly believe that I can complete any task if I set my mind to it.

However, I have come to realize that being independent of parents, siblings, and friends is different from being independent of God. No matter how alone I feel or how unmanageable a task may seem, God is always right beside me, helping me—whether I know it or not.

God lends a helping hand. Am I willing to be dependent on God and to accept God's help? I try to be.

Sylvia C. Dulaney, 17 [Shelbina, Missouri]

5-Second Prayer: God, in my struggle for independence, help me never to push you away. Amen.

For we are what he has made us, created in Christ Jesus for good works, which God prepared beforehand to be our way of life.

Ephesians 2:10 (NRSV)

All of Life Prepares You for What's Ahead

The day I received my first college acceptance letter, I was ready to pack my bags and leave home. I was excited about having no curfew, coming and going as I pleased, and not having Mom and Dad constantly asking me questions. College meant freedom.

As I began my first week of college classes, I realized that I had taken my parents' love and support for granted. Three weeks into the school year, I called my family, sobbing. I missed my life at home, I was overwhelmed by work, and I was battling shyness. Everything and everyone was new. I had the freedom I had been craving, but I missed talking to my parents and depending on their wisdom.

"Can I just come home?" I begged.

Mom answered, "No. You're grown-up. We know you can do this."

"How?" I asked.

Dad responded this time. "From the time you were little, we've been teaching you life lessons and asking God to help us lead you."

Mom spoke again, "You think tests are just in the classroom, but they're not. You've been studying life for eighteen years."

My parents were right. I prayerfully made my way through the school year and loved it. The tests haven't always been easy, but with God's grace and my family's help, I am continuing to pass.

Kate Schmelzer, 21 [Arlington Heights, Illinois]

Journal: Remember the journey that has brought you to this moment. What has prepared you for your independence? Write these conversations, relationships, and events—good and bad—in your journal.

[Jesus said,] "Take the yoke I give you. Put it on your shoulders and learn from me."

Matthew 11:29a (CEV)

Don't Go with the Flow

I don't think the bumper sticker "Go with the Flow" would grace God's car. Going with the flow indicates a lack of direction and a need for boundaries. God has a plan for each of us. Sometimes we deliberately turn away from God's plan; more often, we drift away without noticing. Going with the flow may land you at a party that mixes sex, drugs, and alcohol; but it's more likely to lure you to a friend's house for long hours of video games.

Do you guide your life or let it wander? Consider how often you hang out with whoever is around, do whatever is at hand, go with the flow. What would happen if you limited less productive activities in order to practice a skill or cultivate a talent? What boundaries do you need to establish, not to limit your life but to give it direction?

Rachel Plett, 24 [British Columbia, Canada]

[**Try This:** Draw the bumper sticker of your new life. What simple phrase or image best describes your view and feeling about life right now?]

Don't be afraid, for I am with you.
Don't be discouraged, for I am your God.
I will strengthen you and help you.
Isaiah 41:10 (NLT)

Suicide

Sometimes we carry a heavy burden. Our lives spin out of control, and everything looks hopeless. We wonder, *What's the point of doing anything?* We scream at God and ask, "Why?" We might even consider suicide as the only way out. I have been in that frame of mind before, and I don't want to be there again.

Last year, I attempted suicide. Afterward, I came to realize that I needed guidance. Now, with the help of psychotherapy and antidepressants, I am dealing with my problems in a healthy way; and I am much happier.

The trials of the last year have made me a stronger and better person. I relied on God to get me through. I also came to realize that committing suicide is like saying to God, "The life you gave me isn't good enough, so I quit."

The thought of suicide has crossed my mind since then, but now I know that escaping life is not the answer.

Rebecca Bohn, 16 [Barhamsville, Virginia]

Reflect: What in your life needs to slow down or change? To whom can you talk about your feelings?

When the cares of my heart are many,
your consolations cheer my soul.
Psalm 94:19 (NRSV)

Coping

If you are hurting because of a loss, try these suggestions:

- Accept your feelings. You may feel mad, sad, guilty, and relieved—all at the same time.
- Keep a journal. Write about your thoughts and feelings.
- Talk to an adult you trust, someone who will let you talk about your loss as long and as often as you need to.
- Do something useful with your pain. If you've moved away from home, plan your next visit home. If you have broken up with a boyfriend or girlfriend, call some friends to watch a sappy movie and cry it out. If you are struggling with classes, seek out the tutoring center on campus.
- Pray. Tell God how you feel, even if you're angry. God will give you peace and strength.
- Don't give yourself a time limit. After a year or more, you may still feel the hurt. The pain will eventually lessen, but you may feel a sense of loss for some time.
- Make a memory album. Fill a scrapbook with photos or keepsakes. Good memories can often fill the emptiness.

Katrina Cassel [Ray City, Georgia]

[**5-Second Prayer:** God, console me with your love as I try to move forward. Amen.]

> I know, O LORD, that the way of human beings is not in their control, that mortals as they walk cannot direct their steps.
> Jeremiah 10:23 (NRSV)

In God's Hands

Completely handing over my life to God is one of the hardest things for me to do. Like most people, I want to feel in control of my life, even though all our lives would be better in God's hands. We try to accomplish so many things alone, feeling as if we need no help and willing to do whatever it takes to live the way we want to live.

I constantly struggle to give my life to God. I feel that I have a strong relationship with Jesus, yet I'm not willing to put my entire life into God's hands. I know that if I asked, God would take control of my life and turn it into something I could never do on my own. God would help me to let go of resentments and regrets from the past that I continue to hold inside. God would make me stronger and would lead me to choose an appropriate future for my life. I hope, one day, to turn my entire life over to Jesus and to let him work in ways I cannot.

Katie Nannen, 18 [Kennesaw, Georgia]

[
Give God Your Life: It's not easy to give up control, but it is worth it. Each morning, place your life—all of it—in God's hands. Then get out of the way, and see what amazing things can happen!
]

If you do not stand firm in your faith,
you will not stand at all.
Isaiah 7:9b (NIV)

Open to Decide

My great-uncle is from the Netherlands. All of his life, he has taken pride in being open-minded. He is eager to listen to and learn from every new philosophy, theory, or discovery. He is "always learning but never able to acknowledge the truth" (2 Timothy 3:7, NIV). He does not know God.

In a public college, I am constantly challenged to be open-minded. After all, I can't learn if I refuse to consider other points of view. I listen respectfully as people state their opinions, but I pause before I agree or disagree. And before I make a decision about what I believe, I look to the Bible. I like to hear all sides of the story; but no matter how good some arguments sound, I keep in mind 1 Corinthians 1:20b: "Has not God made foolish the wisdom of the world?" I am responsible for what I believe.

God gives us wisdom as we open our minds to listen, but God also gives us the strength to reject ideas that do not come from God.

Cherith Long, 20 [Mansfield, Texas]

[Improve Your Listening: Do you spend more time listening or talking? This week make an effort to listen more than you speak. When you speak, make sure your words are respectful and glorify God.]

The present or the future—all are yours.
1 Corinthians 3:22b (NIV)

Making Dreams a Reality

When I think about myself in the future, I imagine that I will be well-dressed, in control, and completely content with my life. I imagine myself with a great job, a group of friends, a family, and a close relationship with God. When I imagine the future, everything is positive; and the things I don't like about myself have been magically transformed.

Imagination is great, but it doesn't accomplish much. Hard work is the only way to meet my goals for the future. If I want a great career, I need to develop a responsible work ethic and make good grades. If my dreams are more specific (for instance, I have always wanted to teach English as a second language), I should start learning and preparing now for that particular job. And if having a strong relationship with Christ in the future is important to me, I need to build a firm foundation now through prayer, daily devotions, and being involved with my church and a supportive group of Christian friends.

One of the best things about the future is its uncertainty. No one can control the future; but if I want to accomplish my goals, then I should start working toward them now.

Amanda Southall, 23 [Richmond, Virginia]

Prayer: O God, let me see my future through your eyes and work now to make those dreams come true. Amen.

How much longer, LORD, will you forget about me? . . .
How long must I be confused and miserable all day?
Psalm 13:1–2a (CEV)

Locked by Life

Confusion,
intrusion
is eating my brain.
It's a shame there's no claim to my feelings within.

There's just darkness, and I'm lurking—
a creature without a plan.
In the shadows I'm blind.
I need something to find;
but I'm left without a trace or a clue,
not knowing what's coming,
not knowing what's through.

I'm on the brink—
just need time to think
of ways I can live, but I'm dying.

God, help me now.
I'm patient but intense,
crying but dry,
empty but full
of weirdness.

I miss not knowing right from wrong,
not thinking of things that put beat to a song
when the deep feelings within
begin to penetrate my soul.

Give me a way out; show me the door.
Push me right out
and tell me some more.
The night brings so many things into sight,
but I can't see them without a light.

Taylor Vosler, 17 [Dublin, Ohio]

The Light That You Need
I said to the man who stood
    at the Gate of the Year,
"Give me a light that I may
    go into the unknown."
He said, "Put your hand into
    the hand of God. That is
    light enough."

Edna Chilembo, 18 [Ndola, Zambia]

[Jesus] has been raised from death.

Luke 24:6b (CEV)

Dancing on the Edge

The day I graduated from high school, I realized that it was time for me to grow up. All summer long I was so anxious and excited. I couldn't wait to get to college!

But then the first three months of college life were so depressing. I was really stressed out. I asked myself over and over again, *Why did I choose a college 1,800 miles away from home?*

I stopped going to classes, and I felt that no one even cared. I cried night and day; and sometimes I thought about giving up on my future and on myself. My life was in crisis. I was standing at a crossroads, seeing nowhere to turn and no one to turn to.

It was then that God said to me, "I am standing at the crossroads with you; you are not alone."

No matter what you're going through, remember that God is always there for you, and God wants the best for you. I now realize that God is my rock, my foundation, my cornerstone. I will continue to praise God's name. With God all things are possible.

Vivian Bright, 19 [Miami, Florida]

[

Something to Remember: Christ, who was able to face the cross, can give you the strength to face anything and to share his strength with others.

]

LOOKING AHEAD

As you read, pray, and look ahead, imagine your first step into your new world beyond high school. You have reflected on your past, appreciated the present, and now you have new dreams and visions for the future. Will you step forward cautiously, testing the waters? Will you step forward boldly? Or will you dance with joy?

This is not your last new beginning. The journey of faith is a cycle of listening, learning, and living. But may you always trust in God's love, know you are beloved of God, and obey the promptings of the Holy Spirit. Enjoy the journey!

Waiting can be difficult, but waiting for God is worth it. Check out Lamentations 3:22-26.

Passions for God's Purpose

As a college freshman, I am asked repeatedly, "What's your major?" and "What will you do after you graduate?" These questions can be annoying, but they have led me to look closely at the gifts and passions God has given me.

I have always loved children; I rarely hesitate to baby-sit, tutor, or work with kids on mission trips or at church. I get excited about the chance to make a difference in their lives. My other strong interest is languages—I love Spanish!

I am currently studying elementary education and Spanish to prepare myself to use both of my gifts. Now that I can answer "What's your major?" with confidence, I am waiting patiently for God to reveal how I can best use my passions for God's purpose.

Kathryn Sheffield, 20 [Kennesaw, Georgia]

Wait with Confidence
I search for what is calling me,
where it is that I should go;
and as I search through God's great love,
to solitude I go.

Search through life, knowing that
you can't make it on your own.
Within the silence, talk to God;
and know God's love is home.

Ian Kraft, 20 [Burke, Virginia]

He Walks with Us

I recently read the story of the disciples on the road to
Emmaus in Luke 24:13-35. Shortly after the Crucifixion, two
of Jesus' followers were traveling to Emmaus. It is easy to see
from their conversation the hopelessness and despair that
they felt because of Jesus' death. Whom would they follow
now? Along the road, Jesus appeared and walked with them,
but they did not recognize him. They urged him to stay with
them for the night and later discovered his identity.

The story is about God's faithfulness. When the disciples
were lost in grief, unsure of where to go or what to do, Jesus
walked beside them.

We are a lot like those two disciples. We sometimes feel
hopeless and overburdened. We get so caught up in our own
lives and our own feelings that we do not see what is right
beside us. Jesus walks with us too. When we least expect him
and even when we don't recognize him, Jesus walks with us.

In the next week, be aware of the awesome power of
Jesus in your life. Urge him to stay, and enjoy his company.
And remember, as we travel the road of life, Christ never
fails to surprise us with his presence.

Amy Treece, 24 [Charlotte, North Carolina]

Prayer: Loving Christ, make us aware of your presence,
and slow us down long enough to enjoy your
company. Amen.

The LORD has bared his holy arm
    before the eyes of all the nations;
and all the ends of the earth shall see
    the salvation of our God.

Isaiah 52:10 (NRSV)

Hope for All the Nations

I often argue with my government teacher about politics and current events. Every day he tells the class about another negative news story. He says that in the near future, current events will collide in one huge worldwide catastrophe. He backs up his opinions with information from news broadcasts and magazines. But I don't believe his theories. I don't think civilization will cease to exist just because the news says so.

One day my teacher asked why I thought everything would be fine. Embarrassed, I told him that I did not have credible news sources, books, or other evidence to disprove his theories. What I had was hope, the hope and knowledge that God is in control.

Now I realize that I don't need the latest news reports or the most recent newsmagazines to back up my ideas. All I need is God's Word. My teacher's vast knowledge of current events and his theories of impending doom no longer intimidate me. I feel happy and hopeful knowing that the world is in God's hands.

Joshua Conway, 19 [Altoona, Pennsylvania]

[
Reflect: Set your hope in God, for no matter what troubles beset you, God always has your best interests at heart. **K. S. Hardy** [Bowling Green, Ohio]
]

May the LORD now show you kindness and faithfulness, and I too will show you the same favor.

2 Samuel 2:6a (NIV)

Everyday Blessings

It was one of those days! A test in one class caused me to miss another class. Afterward, as I headed down the hall, I heard someone call my name. I turned to see the teacher of the class I had missed.

I apologized as I fumbled through my backpack and handed him my midterm paper. He graciously took the paper and told me not to worry about missing the class. Then with a smile and a wave, he headed out the door.

On my way home, I thought about that chance meeting, without which my midterm paper would have been late. I realized that God blesses us every day through the people around us—the teachers, family members, friends, pastors, and leaders who make a world of difference in our lives.

Later, in my quiet time, I read 2 Samuel 2:6, in which David thanks the people who have buried King Saul, telling them that God will bless them and that he will show them favor as well. This verse taught me a new way to respond to the kindness of others: I can ask God to bless those who bless me. Praying God's blessings on others is a tremendous gift that we can give, and I believe those who receive it will see Christ in our thankful response to everyday blessings.

David Brandon, 22   [Upland, California]

[
Ask God to Bless Others: Throughout the day, pause to give thanks and to pray God's blessings upon those who bless your life every day.
]

> My comfort in my suffering is this:
> Your promise preserves my life.
> **Psalm 119:50 (NIV)**

Winter and Spring

During the winter of my freshman year in college, I knew how Job must have felt when he questioned his undeserved suffering. Day after day, ashen skies and bitter cold seemed to reflect my doubt and cynicism. Like Job, I was tested as I had never been in my comfortable, predictable life.

I had no idea where I was headed in life and no sense of God's purpose for me. In my religion course, I was questioning my beliefs, dissecting long-held convictions and exposing them to new ways of thinking. I realized that behind a facade of religious obedience I had been hiding a rather flimsy faith. What I thought was a firm foundation of faith was weakened to the point of collapse.

Then I remembered what my grandfather had said to me before I left home—that college would destroy my faith only to rebuild it from the ground up, making the foundations stronger than ever before.

Encouraged, I stumbled on through my winter despair, knowing that my faith would never grow if it were not challenged. College has opened my eyes to the chinks in my faith; it has allowed me to let go of the superficial, to stop simply going through the motions, and to start rebuilding a durable, more genuine faith. As the return of warm sunshine melts the snow and brings new growth, my faith has been renewed.

Evan Hall, 20 [Luck, Wisconsin]

5-Second Prayer: God, be with me in the winter of my faith. Amen.

When God Calls

The Great Pyramid, dinosaur bones, and colonial artifacts: these things intrigued me greatly as a teen. But during my sophomore year of college, I decided not to become an archeologist and instead took secretarial classes. After graduation, I followed that career path.

Years later, I felt God calling me to become a writer. What a surprise that God would inspire me to make a career change when I was happy with what I was doing. However, since I loved to write and the desire was so intense, I was confident that the idea was from God. So, I went back to school and pursued a new career.

I know now that I'm doing what I'm supposed to be doing, and I've never regretted accepting what I felt was a call from God.

These days, young adults feel a lot of pressure about career decisions. And while it is important to have goals and to get a good education, it's also important to be open to God's call, no matter when it happens or where it takes us.

God knows us, loves us, and plans for us "a future with hope." Sometimes our plans change. But by staying open to God's calls, we can be sure to find some wonderful surprises along the way!

Nancy Otto Boffo [Titusville, Florida]

Reflect: Would a change in your path cause anxiety or excitement? Imagine holding your future in your open palm, neither clutching nor dropping. What would you allow God to take from your future? What might God put in its place?

> Whoever wants to become great among you must be your servant, and whoever wants to be first must be your slave.
> **Matthew 20:26-27 (NIV)**

What Was Jesus Thinking?

Servant Leadership

Think about the people you know at school or at work. Who is striving to be "great among you"? Think about the world. Who wants to be a world leader? Who wants to be first? How do class officers, student government leaders, governors, and presidents become leaders? Some are popular. Some are wealthy. Some are born at the right time, in the right place, and among the right people. Some are elected. Not many are servants.

Maybe times have changed since Jesus spoke. Certainly our ideas about leadership have changed. America continues to reinvent its understanding of leadership. Many books have been written about how to become a great leader. One popular idea about leadership is summed up in this philosophy: "Work smart, not hard." I don't think Jesus would agree. This is not what Jesus had in mind when he spoke of personal greatness.

When I work with student leaders, I look for people who are willing to work hard. And even more importantly, I look for people with passion, who are concerned about the people they serve. I look for servant leaders.

So what was Jesus thinking when he spoke the words recorded in Matthew 20:26-27? Jesus knew that as we serve others, we learn. We recognize our gifts and talents by using them to benefit others. We break down barriers between those we serve and ourselves. And as we look for ways to serve God, we begin to see the greatness God created in each of us.

You Can Lead Now!

According to Jesus, you can be a leader right now. You don't need to be elected. Issues of popularity, heritage, or economics don't matter. Only your attitude and your willingness to serve others are important.

Jesus says that if someone wants to be a leader, he or she must first become a servant. The first step in becoming a leader is asking, "Where does God want me to serve? Whom shall I serve?" Look for places where you can lead—at home, at school, at church, at work, on the athletic field. Every day, God gives us opportunities to serve.

Is Jesus' style of leadership appropriate for our generation? Try it out. As you begin to serve, you will be presented with more and more opportunities for servant leadership.

Mike Nygren [Tipp City, Ohio]

Pray a Prayer of the Church:
Teach us, good Lord,
to serve you as you deserve;
to give and not to count the cost;
to fight and not to heed the wounds;
to toil and not to seek for rest;
to labor and not to ask for any reward,
except that of knowing that we do your will;
through Jesus Christ our Lord. Amen.

—Ignatius of Loyola, Spain, 16th century

In this world you will have trouble. But take heart! I have overcome the world.

John 16:33b (NIV)

The Joy of the Lord

Thoughtful, melancholy, artistic—that's me. Of course, the shadow side of these qualities means I can also be self-centered, pessimistic, or flat-out depressed. Since I'm prone to personal pits, I'm realizing my need to cultivate joy.

In Nehemiah 8:10b (NRSV), God says, "The joy of the LORD is your strength." The Jews in Nehemiah's day had good reason to be sad, but God commanded them to cheer up. Knowing that prolonged sadness makes us weak, both inside and out, God told the Jews to throw a party, to eat great food, and to enjoy themselves. Living in "the joy of the Lord" is not always about experiencing a spiritual high. Sometimes it's about *choosing* to be happy.

When Jesus said good-bye to his disciples, he told them that things would get bad, that they would face persecution and failure; but he also assured them that they could be at peace and have good cheer because he had overcome the world.

A lot of difficult things happen in life. My days are often full of trouble. Yet Jesus has overcome the world! So I have a reason to be cheerful. I don't have to stay down; I can choose to be an optimist.

Rachel Starr Thomson [Ontario, Canada]

Practice Joy: Life is not always one happy event after another; but when bad things happen, we can still trust that we're OK because God is with us. That's joy—a deep feeling of well-being no matter what happens. Joy doesn't happen instantly; it comes through practice. Begin today by asking God to help you cultivate an attitude of joy.

Richard Lawton [Adelaide, Australia]

Choose Joy!

Psalm 16:8-11   Psalm 47:1-2   Psalm 150
Psalm 30:11-12   Psalm 63:5-8   John 15:9-11
Psalm 45.7   Psalm 98

Think About This: Things will go wrong at times. You can't always control circumstances. However, you can always control your attitude, approach, and response.

Tony Dungy

Professor Jordan

I stared at my grade and read Dr. Jordan's note: "See me after class." The assignment had included this odd final question: "How are you doing personally?" I had written about feeling lonely, since this was my first semester in college; but I had forgotten about this question until now.

As I stood in front of her desk, she said, "I thought you might like to get together for coffee. How does tomorrow work for you?"

I nodded. "That would be nice."

The next day, Dr. Jordan and I sat in a cozy café and talked. I opened up about my life. She listened, asked me questions, and offered me counsel and advice. I felt refreshed.

By my sophomore year, I didn't hesitate to plop into the chair in Dr. Jordan's office. Since our first meeting, we've shared our prayer requests, written each other notes, and enjoyed an occasional lunch together. In a sense, I have viewed her not only as a teacher and a mentor but also as a mom-away-from-home. I chose my college for its strength in my intended field of study. I didn't realize that God would bless me with a wise and godly mentor too.

Kate Elise Gutierrez, 23 [Arlington Heights, Illinois]

What Is a Mentor?

One who guides me on the path yet to come,
one who points out the stones on which I could
    stumble,
one who urges me to continue when I become weary
    of the walk,
one who shares the journey with me.

K. S. Hardy [Bowling Green, Ohio]

Reflect: Do you have a mentor—someone older
that you trust and can talk to about anything? If not,
pray about someone in your church (or school or
workplace) who might be a good mentor for you.

Crystal Mazzuca [Olympia, Washington]

Mary said:
With all my heart I praise the Lord,
and I am glad because of God my Savior.
Luke 1:46-47 (CEV)

Welcome to the Dance

As we walk through life, desperately seeking God's guidance, we often find ourselves stumbling over stones in the path or halting our journey at every crossroad. And yet somehow, we keep walking.

When I was in first grade, a friend told me that she found it easier and more fun to skip than to walk. Perhaps if we skipped or danced to our destinations, life would be less about how we stumble over the rocks and more about the rhythmic moving of our feet, dancing to the glory of our Lord.

This journey that God has allowed us to take is a celebration, and all are invited. Psalm 150:4a (CEV) tells us to "praise [God] with tambourines and dancing." Let's celebrate! Whatever our tasks, rather than just putting one foot in front of the other to get them done, let's dance our way to getting them accomplished, knowing that God dances with us. Then life will be a dance leading all the way to eternal life with God; and we'll be skipping, hopping, or jumping over every boulder or tiny pebble that is thrown into our path.

Lisette Johnson, 16 [Cincinnati, Ohio]

5-Second Prayer: Dear Lord, dance with me on the road of life, teaching me the steps and lifting me when I fall. Amen.

About the Compiler

Kara Lassen Oliver, a graduate of Vanderbilt Divinity School, began her ministry at the United Methodist Youth Organization, where she discovered a love for and commitment to the questions of young people. This passion led her to the local church, where she served as a youth pastor for two years.

Kara is the author of *Stepping into the World Participant's Book*, volume 5 in The Way of Pilgrimage series for youth and young adults. She and her husband, Jeff, and their two children are currently serving with Volunteers in Mission in Malawi. For more information, see Kara's blog at blog.oliverville.org.

If you enjoyed the devotions in this book, consider subscribing to **devozine**, a devotional lifestyle magazine.

Order online: www.devozine.org
Order by phone: 1-800-972-0433